The Ultimate Spanish Cookbook

Cookbook

111 best Spanish dishes to cook right now

Slavka Bodic

Introduction

Many dishes in Spain are prepared today using the same ingredients and cooking methods as they were employed 300 years ago. Like the Romans, the Arabs who conquered and lived in Spain for eight centuries years made a significant impact to Spanish cuisine, as evident in various recipes within this cookbook. Other dishes originated from neighboring European countries, while American recipes and methods were adapted to the Spanish taste.

The two basic ingredients of all Spanish food are garlic and olive oil. Accordingly, I'm using these two ingredients a lot in my home country, because I simply adore Spanish food. However, because Spain has very distinct geographical regions settled by different ethnic groups, the regional cuisines vary drastically. While you can easily identify what is Greek cuisine, Spain is more similar to Italy, where each region has its own cuisine. Spanish cuisine is a diverse fusion of many excellent meals, but many times the only common ingredients involve olive oil and garlic.

My family members adore stew, so I find so many terms that people and communities in Spain use (Pote, Escudella, Cocido, Olla, Guiso, Estofado, etc.). I'm sure you'll enjoy preparing all of them. If you like to roast, fry, and sauté, then this cuisine is also ideal for you. Baking and broiling aren't common methods.

Besides, Spanish cuisine is well-known around the globe and some of its specialties are so popular that you must try them on your next trip to Spain. Besides the food, please don't forget to visit Alhambra in Granada. All the recipes I presented are renowned, so you can easily find local ingredients in neighboring shops. Moreover, I selected recipes that are easy to make within limited time.

Traditional Spanish cuisine is down-to-earth, uncomplicated food based on the ingredients available locally or the crops grown regionally.

As the Spanish say to wish people a good meal, "Buen provecho!"

Table of Contents

Breakfast

Spanish Cheese and Potato Omelet

Preparation time: 20 minutes

Cook time: 70 minutes

Nutrition fact (per serving): 512 kcal (20 oz. protein, 20 oz. fat, 40 oz. of carbohydrates)

Ingredients (4 servings)

2 lbs. potatoes

1 onion

1 garlic clove

1 tablespoon olive oil

1 can tomatoes

Salt and cayenne pepper to taste

Sweet paprika powder

1 teaspoon sugar

1 tablespoon wine vinegar

7 oz. red pepper

5 ½ oz. pitted green olives

8 stems thyme

1 egg

2 tablespoons milk

5 ¼ oz. sour cream

3 oz. grated Gouda cheese

Pepper to taste

8 slices Serrano ham

Preparation

Wash the potatoes and boil for 22 minutes. Peel the onion and 1 clove of garlic and dice finely. Heat the oil and sauté the onion and garlic for about 3 minutes while stirring. Add the tomatoes and remove the pot from the stove. Finely chop them with the hand blender. Season them to your taste with salt, cayenne pepper, paprika powder, sugar, and wine vinegar. Chill the sauce.

Clean, wash, and finely dice the peppers. Slice olives. Rinse the potatoes under cold water, drain the water, and remove the peel. Cut the potatoes into slices. Wash thyme, shake dry, pick off the leaves. Peel and finely dice the remaining garlic. Whisk the eggs, milk, sour cream, cheese, thyme and garlic. Season with salt and pepper. Mix the diced paprika, olive slices, and egg mixture and place in a greased pizza tray (approximately 12.2 inches diameter).

Bake in a warmed-up oven (electric stove: 390 ° F/ convection: 350 ° F) for 42-46 minutes. Remove the finished omelet from the oven, let it rest briefly, and cut it into pieces like cake. Arrange the omelet, sauce, and ham on plates. Sprinkle with thyme.

Spanish Tomato Omelet

Preparation time: 20 minutes

Cook time: 40 minutes

Nutrition fact (per serving): 290 kcal (½ oz. protein, 20 oz. fat, ¼ oz. of carbohydrates)

Ingredients (4 servings)

18 oz. medium-sized tomatoes

2 large onions

½ pot of fresh or 2 teaspoons of dried oregano

6 eggs

¾ cup milk

4 thin slices of bacon (bacon)

4 teaspoons of oil

Salt and white pepper to taste

Preparation

Wash, clean, and slice the tomatoes. Peel, cut in half, and slice the onions. Wash the oregano and then pull off the leaves. Put some aside for garnish. Whisk the eggs and milk together. Season with salt, pepper, and oregano.

Cut the bacon into strips. Fry in a pan (approximately 1-inch diameter) without fat until crispy and then remove. Heat 1 teaspoon of oil in the bacon fat. Cook 1/4 onions in it. Put ¼ tomato slices in and sauté. Pour in ¼ of the egg milk. Cover and let stand for about 11 minutes over low to medium heat. Keep warm. Prepare 3 more omelets in the same way; keep warm. Sprinkle the omelets with bacon and garnish with oregano.

Pickled Sheep's Cheese with Herbs

Preparation time: 20 minutes

Cook time: 30 minutes

Nutrition fact (per serving): 252 kcal (10 oz. protein, 10 oz. fat, 1 ounce of carbohydrates)

Ingredients (4 servings)

5 stems thyme and oregano

3 stems basil

1 red onion

1 clove of garlic

1 small, green hot pepper

1 tablespoon olive oil

14 oz. sheep's cheese

Preparation

Wash all herbs and shake dry. Detach the leaves from the stems and chop them. Peel the onion and cut it into rings. Peel and finely dice the garlic. Wash and clean the peppers and cut into fine rings. Mix the herbs, pepperoni, onion, garlic, and oil. Cut the cheese into cubes and marinate with the prepared herb oil for about 30 minutes. Arrange in a bowl.

Spanish Asparagus Plate

Preparation time: 60 minutes

Cook time: 90 minutes

Nutrition fact (per serving): 324 kcal (½ oz. protein, 1 oz. fat, ¼ oz. of carbohydrates)

Ingredients (4 servings)

2 ½ lbs. white asparagus

2 pinches of sugar

2 teaspoon lemon juice

1 egg

1 teaspoon medium-hot mustard

1 tablespoon white wine vinegar

½ cup oil

13 oz. skimmed milk yogurt

1 clove of garlic

1 rosemary, thyme, and basil stems

1 beefsteak tomato

4 peppercorns

120 oz. Spanish serrano ham (thinly sliced)

1 basil, lemon, and caper apple

1 onion

Salt to taste

Preparation

Clean the asparagus and cut the hard ends. Cook the asparagus in boiling salted water with a pinch of sugar and lemon juice for 18-20 minutes. Mix the egg, salt, mustard, and vinegar with a cutting stick. Gradually beat in the oil. Stir in the yogurt. Season to taste. Peel the garlic. Wash herbs, shake dry. Chop everything and stir in 1/3 of the mayonnaise.

Peel and chop the onion. Wash, clean, core, and finely dice the tomatoes and crush peppercorns. Stir everything into the second third of the mayonnaise. Lift the asparagus from the water and let it cool down. Wrap with the ham. Serve with the mayonnaise and garnish with basil, lemon, and caper apples. Pair a baguette or farmer's bread with it.

Spanish Tomato Omelet

Preparation time: 55 minutes

Cook time: 30 minutes

Nutrition fact (per serving): 323 kcal (½ oz. protein, 20 oz. fat, ¼ oz. of carbohydrates)

Ingredients (4 servings)

18 oz. tomatoes

2 onions

6 eggs

¾ cup of milk

Dried or fresh oregano

4 slices breakfast bacon (bacon)

4 tablespoon olive oil

Salt and pepper to taste

Preparation

Wash, clean, and slice tomatoes. Peel, cut in half, and slice the onions. Whisk the eggs and milk together. Season with salt, pepper, and oregano. Cut the bacon into pieces. Fry in a pan with no fat until crispy. Steam ¼ of the onion slices in 1 tablespoon of oil until translucent. Add ¼ of the tomato slices. Pour ¼ of the egg-milk and cover; next, let stand for about 10 minutes.

Finally, sprinkle some pieces of bacon over the top and heat it up. Do the same with the remaining vegetables, egg milk, and bacon. Sprinkle fresh oregano over the omelets, if you like.

Omelet With Potatoes, Onions and Hot Peppers

Preparation time: 25 minutes

Cook time: 20 minutes

Nutrition fact (per serving): 562 kcal (21 oz. protein, 3 oz. fat, 15 oz. of carbohydrates)

Ingredients (4 servings)

4 tablespoons of extra virgin olive oil

27 oz. potatoes, halved lengthways, sliced

2 onions, sliced

1 red peppers, pitted and diced

6 eggs

1 pinch freshly ground pepper

1 pinch coarse sea salt

2 green peppers, cut into small pieces

Preparation

Heat 2 tablespoon of oil in a large, heavy pan. Add the potatoes, halved lengthways, and sliced. Add the onions, cut into fine slices, and chopped peppers before cooking over medium heat for 26-32 minutes. Turn occasionally, cover for the last 10 minutes.

Lightly beat the eggs, salt, and pepper in a large bowl. Use a slotted spoon to lift the potatoes into the bowl and stir briefly. Heat 1 tablespoon of oil in the pan, add the potato and egg mixture, and reduce the heat. After about 5-6 minutes, the omelet is whipped and fried until golden.

Place on an oiled plate and turn back into the pan, top first. Let the remaining oil run down the edge of the pan and under the omelet; let it set and brown for another 5 minutes over high heat. Allow it to cool down a bit on a cake plate.

Spanish Potato Omelet

Preparation time: 90 minutes

Cook time: 30 minutes

Nutrition Fact (per serving): 544 kcal (1 oz. protein, 10 1/2 oz. fat, 10 oz. of carbohydrates)

Ingredients (4 servings)

2 lbs. potatoes

1 onion

1 garlic clove

1 tablespoon olive oil

1 can of tomato

1 cayenne pepper

1 sweet paprika

1 tablespoon white wine vinegar

1 red pepper

3 ½ oz. pitted green olives

3 oz. Manchego

5 stems thyme

1 egg

7 tablespoon milk

7 oz. sour cream

Salt to taste

Preparation

Wash the potatoes and cook covered for about 20 minutes. Quench, peel, and let cool. Peel and finely dice the onion and garlic. Heat the oil in the pan. Sauté the onion and half of the garlic until translucent. Add the tomatoes with their juice and then bring to the boil and puree. Season to taste with salt, cayenne pepper, paprika powder, a little sugar, and vinegar.

Clean, wash, and finely dice the peppers. Slice the olives and the potatoes. Grate the cheese. Wash and pluck thyme. Whisk both with eggs, milk, sour cream, and the rest of the garlic. Season with salt and pepper vigorously.

Mix the potatoes, peppers, olives and egg mixture. Place in a greased pizza tray (12-inch diameter). Bake in a preheated oven at 390 ° F for about 45 minutes. Take out, let rest briefly, and then cut into pieces. Serve with tomato sauce, Serrano ham, and olives.

Zucchini and Ham Rolls

Preparation time: 30 minutes

Cook time: 30 minutes

Nutrition fact (per serving): 120 kcal (¼ oz. protein, 1 oz. fat, ¼ oz. of carbohydrates)

Ingredients (4 servings)

2 zucchinis

2 tablespoon Sherry vinegar

4 tablespoon olive oil

1 teaspoon oregano, chopped

1 pinch salt

1 pinch black pepper

1 clove of garlic

12 thin serrano ham

3 oz. Iberic cheese

Preparation

Wash the zucchini, clean, pat dry, and cut lengthways into 6 thin strips. Blanch the strips in hot, salted water for about 2 minutes, place in a sieve, rinse in cold water, and allow them to cool. Mix the sherry vinegar, olive oil, oregano, salt, and pepper together. Squeeze the garlic and add to the sauce. Split the ham slices lengthways in half and then grate the cheese finely. Spread the zucchini strips flat, pat dry, brush with the sauce, and cover each with a halved slice of ham. Sprinkle the cheese on top. Roll up the vegetables and pin the zucchini with toothpicks.

Stuffed Zucchini

Preparation time: 25 minutes

Cooking time: 35 minutes

Nutrition fact (per serving): 160 kcal (¼ oz. protein, 1 oz. fat, ½ oz. of carbohydrates)

Ingredients (4 servings)

2 small zucchinis

2 oz. white bread

2 oz. Serrano ham, thin slices

2 garlic cloves

2 oz. Emmentaler cheese

1 egg

2 tablespoon Parsley, chopped, smooth

1 pinch salt

1 pinch black pepper

1 tablespoon olive oil

1 oz. grated Manchego

Preparation

Wash and clean the zucchini, remove the stems, cut in half lengthways, and remove the seeds. Soak the bread in warm water, squeeze it out and chop it finely. Cut the ham into fine strips. Peel the garlic and chop into fine slithers. Dice the cheese.

Preheat the oven to 390 ° F. Mix the bread, strips of ham, garlic, cheese cubes, egg, and parsley together well. Salt and pepper the mixture and pour into the zucchini halves. Grease a large baking dish with 1 tablespoon of olive oil, put the zucchini in it, and sprinkle with the Manchego. Drizzle with the remaining oil. Baked the zucchini on the middle rack in the oven for about 36 minutes. Finally, cut into pieces.

Tortilla De Gambas

Preparation time: 35 minutes

Cooking time: 10 minutes

Nutrition fact (per serving): 330 kcal (¼ ounce protein, 10 oz. fat, 1 ounce of carbohydrates)

Ingredients (4 servings)

22 oz. deep-sea prawns

1 lemon, juice from it

1 pinch salt

2 garlic cloves

3 tablespoon olive oil for the pan

6 eggs

1 pinch black pepper

Preparation

Place the prawns in a bowl, drizzle with lemon juice, season with salt and pepper. Peel the garlic, press over it (garlic press), and mix everything well. Heat a dash of olive oil in a pan and briefly toss the shrimp in it.

Now whisk the eggs in a bowl, season with salt and pepper, and pour evenly over the prawns into the pan. Let it set over mild heat for about 6 minutes. Then slide the finished tortilla de gambas onto a plate and cut into pieces of cake or bite-sized cubes.

Appetizers and Dips

Bacon Tapas with Sea Salt Potatoes

Preparation time: 60 minutes

Cook time: 30 minutes

Nutrition fact (per serving): 632 kcal (½ oz. protein, 1½ oz. fat, 40 oz. of carbohydrates)

Ingredients (4 servings)

2 lbs. small potatoes

4 tablespoons olive oil

1 ½ teaspoon sea salt

2 garlic cloves

10 ½ oz. whole milk yogurt

2 tablespoon salad mayonnaise

1 oz. stuffed olives

16 slices bacon

16 (approximately 3 ½ oz.) dried soft tomatoes

1 bunch chives

2 tablespoon oil

Lettuce leaves and olives

Salt and pepper to taste

16 wooden skewers

Preparation

Preheat the oven (electric stove: 390 ° F/ convection: 350 ° F). Wash the potatoes thoroughly and pat dry. Mix with olive oil and 1 teaspoon of coarse salt. Put on a baking sheet. Bake in the hot oven for 45–55 minutes until cooked.

For the dip, peel and roughly chop the garlic, sprinkle with a little salt and mash with a fork. Mix the yogurt, mayonnaise, and garlic together. Season with a bit of salt and pepper. Wrap the olives with 1 slice of bacon each. Wrap 2 dried tomatoes with 1 slice of bacon each. Wash the chives, shake dry and cut into large rolls.

Heat the oil in a pan. Fry the bacon olives and bacon tomatoes until crispy while turning. Put on skewers and arrange on lettuce leaves with olives. Remove the potatoes from the oven, season again with ½ teaspoon of coarse salt, and sprinkle with chives. Serve the potatoes and aioli dip with the skewers.

Snack Tuna Empanadas
with Mojo Verde

Preparation time: 55 minutes

Cook time: 80 minutes

Nutrition fact (per serving): 580 kcal, (½ oz. protein, 3 oz. fat, 6 oz. of carbohydrates)

Ingredients (8 servings)

3 oz. cold butter

23 oz. flour

1 egg

1 pinch salt

1 pinch turmeric

1 tablespoon white wine vinegar

1 can (7 oz.) tuna in oil

1 spring onion

1 packet ground saffron

1 small bunch coriander

1 small bunch parsley

2 garlic cloves

1 organic lemon

6 tablespoon olive oil

1 teaspoon sugar

1 egg yolk

Pepper to taste

1 tablespoon whipped cream

3 cups flour

1 foil

Preparation

Cut the butter into cubes. Knead the flour and butter with your hands until crumbly. Add egg, 2 ½ fluid oz. of lukewarm water, 1 pinch of salt, turmeric, and vinegar to the flour. First, knead with the hand mixer's dough hook, then with your hands to form smooth dough. Wrap the dough in foil and put it in the fridge for about 30 minutes. Drain the tuna well and tear it apart. Wash the spring onions and slice it into fine rings. Mix the tuna, spring onions, and saffron, season with salt and pepper.

Wash the coriander and parsley, shake dry, pluck the leaves from the stems and, with the exception of a few for garnish, roughly shred. Peel and roughly chop the garlic. Wash and clean the lemon with hot water, rub dry, peel off the peel, and squeeze it out of the lemon. Finely puree the herbs, garlic, lemon juice, zest, oil, and sugar in a tall container with a cutting—stick season to taste with salt and pepper.

Whisk egg yolks with cream. Knead the dough again with your hands. Roll out the dough for about 1/8 inches thin on a floured work surface and cut out circles (approximately 3 inch in diameter). Cut out a total of approximately 24 circles, knead the remnants of the dough, and roll out again until the dough is used up.

Place approximately 1 teaspoon of the tuna filling on circular dough, brush the edges with egg yolk, and fold half of the dough over the filling so that a semicircle is created. Press the edges well and form a cord edge.

Brush the empanadas with the egg yolk mix and spread on 1-2 baking sheets lined with baking paper. Bake in a pre-heated oven (electric stove: 390 ° F or convectional: 350 ° F) for 27 minutes or until golden brown. Take empanadas out of the oven, let them cool down a bit, arrange on a plate, and garnish with the rest of the herb leaves. Serve with mojo verde.

Pear in Serrano Ham

Preparation time: 20 minutes

Cook time: 10 minutes

Nutrition fact (per serving): 152 kcal (½ ounce protein, ¼ ounce fat, ½ ounce of carbohydrates)

Ingredients (4 servings)

1 organic lemon

1 ripe pear

12 thin slices Serrano ham

Wooden skewers

Preparation

Cut the lemon into halve and squeeze out the juice. Mix lemon juice with 1¾ fluid oz. water. Peel and halve the pears, remove the core, and cut each half into 6 wedges. Place the pear wedges in the lemon water.

Halve each ham slices lengthways. Remove the pear wedges from the lemon water and drain on some kitchen paper. Wrap each pear wedge in 1 piece of ham and secure with a wooden skewer. Chill until serving.

Tapas Skewers "En Garde" with Aioli and Chorizo

Preparation time: 40 minutes

Cook time: 30 minutes

Nutritional facts (per serving): 279 kcal (½ oz. protein, ¾ oz. of fat, ¾ oz. of carbohydrate)

Ingredients (4 servings)
½ pack (10 oz. each) puff pastry (cooling shelf)

1 egg

1 tablespoon milk

1 clove of garlic

4 tablespoon salad cream

20 oz. arugula

8 cherry tomatoes

16 thin slices Chorizo cold cuts

Parchment paper

16 wooden skewers

Preparation

Remove the puff pastry from the refrigerator 10 minutes before use. Line a baking sheet with baking paper. Preheat the oven (electric stove: 390 ° F/ convection: 350 ° F). Whisk the egg and milk together.

Unroll the puff pastry and cut out approximately 16 circles (1-inch diameter) close together. Place on the baking sheet. Brush each circle thinly with egg-milk, avoiding the edges. Bake in the warmed-up oven for about 15 minutes until golden. Take out and let them cool down.

Meanwhile, peel the garlic for the aioli and chop it very finely. Mix with the salad cream. Sort the arugula, wash, and spin dry. Wash tomatoes and cut in half.

Cut each puff pastry circle horizontally with a saw knife. Cover the underside with aioli, 1 folded chorizo slice, 1 tomato half, and a little arugula. Put the puff pastry lid on and fix everything with wooden skewers.

Aioli

Preparation time: 10 minutes

Cook time: 10 minutes

Nutritional facts (per serving): 61 kcal (½ oz. protein, 1 oz. of fat, ½ oz. of carbohydrate)

Ingredients (4 servings)

1 egg yolk (hard-boiled)

1 teaspoon of lemon juice

1 cup olive oil

1 clove of garlic

1 pinch of salt

1 pinch white pepper

1 shot vinegar

Preparation

Mix the hard-boiled egg (chop up) and lemon juice in a bowl. Add the oil drop by drop, constantly stirring, until the mass thickens. Add the remaining oil spoon by spoon, constantly stirring (with a mixer or hand blender). Peel and squeeze the garlic and add to the mayonnaise. Season the sauce with salt, pepper, and a dash of vinegar.

Soups

Spanish Lentil Soup with Chorizo and Paprika

Preparation time: 10 minutes

Cook time: 15 minutes

Nutrition fact (per serving): 572 kcal (20 oz. protein, 30 oz. fat, 20 oz. of carbohydrates)

Ingredients (4 servings)

1 green and red pepper

1 clove of garlic

7 oz. Chorizo sausage

1 tablespoon olive oil

9 oz. red lentils

1 teaspoon instant vegetable broth

1 parsley

7 oz. sour cream

Salt and black pepper to taste

Sweet paprika

Preparation

Clean, wash, and chop the peppers. Peel and dice the garlic. Chop the Chorizo. Heat the oil in a fry pan, fry the Chorizo in it, and remove. Sauté the paprika and garlic in the frying fat. Add the lentils and fry briefly. Remove 5 ½ cups of water. Bring to the boil and simmer for 11-14 minutes. Stir in the broth. Add the sausage and season with salt and pepper. Wash the parsley, pat dry, and roughly chop. Sprinkle over the soup. Serve with sour cream and dust with paprika powder.

Granada Potato Soup

Preparation time: 45 minutes

Cook time: 30 minutes

Nutrition fact (per serving): 640 kcal (30 oz. protein, 30 oz. fat, 30 oz. of carbohydrates)

Ingredients (4 servings)

1 onion

1 clove of garlic

2 lbs. floury potatoes

5 ¼ oz. Chorizo

1 tablespoon oil

5 tablespoon dry sherry

2-3 teaspoon vegetable broth (instant)

salt and pepper to taste

1 red pepper

5 ¼ oz. Manchego (Spanish hard cheese)

4 stems parsley

1 tablespoon almond kernels (e.g. smoked almonds)

3 ½ oz. whipping cream

Preparation

Peel and finely dice the onion and garlic. Peel, wash, and dice the potatoes. Remove the chorizo from the skin and cut into slices. Heat the oil in a pot. Fry the sausage in it and remove it. Fry the garlic and onion in the hot frying fat. Fry the potatoes briefly. Deglaze with sherry, let it almost evaporate. Pour in 4 cups of water, bring to the boil, and stir in the stock. Season with salt and pepper. Cover the soup and simmer for about 20 minutes.

Clean and wash the peppers. Dice the paprika and cheese. Wash and chop the parsley. Roughly chop the almonds. Coarsely mash the potatoes. Refine with cream. Season the soup to taste and serve. Sprinkle with chorizo, paprika, cheese, parsley, and almonds.

Spanish Lentil Soup with Spinach

Preparation time: 60 minutes

Cook time: 55 minutes

Nutrition fact (per serving): 459 kcal (1 ounce protein, 20 oz. fat, 30 oz. of carbohydrates)

Ingredients (4 servings)

2 red peppers

7 oz. Pardina lentils

2 onions

4 garlic cloves

2 tablespoon almond flakes

2 tablespoon olive oil

4 stems thyme

2 bay leaves

1 jar ground saffron

7 oz. whipping cream

2 teaspoon vegetable broth (instant)

3 ½ oz. young spinach

3 oz. dried soft apricots

Grated zest and juice of ½ organic lemon

Salt and pepper to taste

Parchment paper

Preparation

Preheat the oven (electric stove: 480 ° F / convection: 430 ° F). Line a baking sheet with parchment paper. Clean, wash, and quarter the peppers. Prick several times with a wooden skewer or sharp knife. Place on the baking sheet with the skin side up. Roast in the hot oven in the upper third for 12–15 minutes until the skin blisters.

In the meantime, wash the lentils in a sieve with cold water and drain. Cook in boiling water for about 30 minutes. Peel the onions and garlic, chop both finely. Roast the almonds in a saucepan until golden brown and then remove.

Heat the oil in the pan. Sauté the onions and garlic in it. Wash the thyme, shake dry, and pick off the leaves. Add the bay leaves and saffron and fry for about 1 minute. Pour 4 cups of water and cream and bring to boil. Stir in the broth. Simmer open for 10 minutes. Take the peppers out of the oven, cover immediately with a wet kitchen towel and allow them to cool. Peel the peppers and cut into strips. Sort the spinach, wash, and drain well. Cut the apricots into small cubes.

Drain the lentils. Add to the broth with paprika, spinach, apricots, and lemon zest. Bring everything to a boil briefly. Season to taste with approximately 2 tablespoons of lemon juice, salt and pepper. Serve with almonds.

Spanish Tomato Soup
with Meatballs

Preparation time: 30 minutes

Cook time: 60 minutes

Nutrition fact (per serving): 632 kcal (30 oz. protein, 1 ounce of fat, 2 oz. of carbohydrates)

Ingredients (4 servings)

3 lbs. beefsteak tomatoes

Small vegetable onions (9-11 oz.)

4 garlic cloves

14 oz. mixed minced meat

1 egg

4 tablespoon breadcrumbs

8 tablespoon dry sherry

Salt and pepper to taste

1 rose peppers

4 tablespoon olive oil

1 tablespoon tomato paste

1 tablespoon flour

3½ cups clear beef broth (instant)

5¼ oz. long grain rice, parboiled

1 teaspoon sugar

½ bunch flat-leaf parsley

Preparation

Wash, drain, and dice tomatoes. Peel the onion and garlic. Halve the onion, cut off approximately 1/8 and finely dice. Roughly dice the rest of the onion. Press 2 cloves of garlic with a garlic press. Knead the minced meat, egg, breadcrumbs, finely diced onion, garlic, and 3 tablespoons of sherry. Season with salt, pepper, and hot paprika.

Shape walnut-sized meatballs with moistened hands. Heat the oil in a large saucepan and fry the meatballs until golden brown while turning. Remove and sauté the remaining onion cubes. Add the tomatoes and press the remaining garlic cloves through a press and sauté briefly. Season with salt and pepper. Take almost 1/4 of the tomato mixture from the pot and set aside. Stir the tomato paste and flour one after the other into the tomatoes in the saucepan and sauté briefly. Pour in the stock and 5 tablespoons of sherry, bring to the boil, and simmer covered for 35-45 minutes.

Meanwhile, cook rice in salted water according to the instructions on the packet. Puree the finished soup, add the removed tomato mixture again and season with salt, pepper, and sugar. Put the beef broth in the soup, heat again, and let simmer for about 5 minutes. Wash the parsley, pat dry, and cut into strips. Serve the soup with a little rice and sprinkle with parsley.

Spanish Pepper and Tomato Soup

Preparation time: 45 minutes

Cook time: 20 minutes

Nutrition fact (per serving): 168 kcal (¼ oz. protein, 5 oz. fat, ¼ oz. of carbohydrates)

Ingredients (4 servings)

2 red peppers

2 onions

1 clove of garlic

1 tablespoon olive oil

1 can chunky tomatoes

6 tablespoon soy sauce

Salt and pepper to taste

1 pinch sugar

1 tablespoon Creme fraiche cheese

Preparation

Wash and clean the red peppers and cut them into cubes. Peel the onions and garlic and cut into cubes. Heat the oil and stir-fry the prepared vegetables until translucent. Add the tomatoes, soy sauce, and 4 cups of water. Bring to the boil and simmer for about 20 minutes. Finely chop the soup with the hand blender—season to taste with salt, pepper, and sugar. Arrange the soup with 1 tablespoon each of crème fraîche on plates.

Spanish Corn Soup

Preparation time: 50 minutes

Cook time: 40 minutes

Nutrition fact (per serving): 341 kcal (10.32 oz. protein, 10.07 oz. fat, 30.25 oz. of carbohydrates)

Ingredients (4 servings)

7 oz. ground beef

1 egg

3 tablespoon (½ oz. each) tomato paste

1 tablespoon breadcrumbs

Salt and pepper to taste

1 onion

1 tablespoon oil Vegetable broth (instant)

1 packet ground saffron

3 ½ oz. long grain rice

1 (approximately 9 oz.) red pepper

5¼ oz. frozen green beans

7 oz. celery leaves

2 tomatoes (approximately 3 oz. each)

½ can of yellow corn

A few squirts of lemon juice

Sugar to taste

Parchment paper

Preparation

Knead the mince, egg, tomato paste, and breadcrumbs. Next, season well with salt and pepper. Shape the mixture into about 20 balls and place on a baking sheet lined with baking paper. Cook in a warmed-up oven (electric stove: 350 ° F / convectional: 300 ° F) for about 16 minutes. In the meantime, skin and finely dice the onion. Heat the oil in a fry pan and sauté the onion. Deglaze with broth, stir in saffron, and add rice. Cook on medium heat for 20 minutes. In the meantime, quarter the peppers, clean, wash and cut into pieces. Rinse the beans briefly with hot water and let them drain.

Clean, wash, and slice the celery (put some green celery aside). Clean and wash tomatoes and cut them into wedges. Rinse the corn briefly and let it drain. After about 10 minutes, add the vegetables to the rice and cook at the same time. Season the soup with salt, pepper, lemon juice, and a pinch of sugar. Arrange the soup in deep plates, add the chopped balls, and serve garnished with celery leaves.

Gazpacho Soup

Preparation time 20 minutes

Cook time: 15 minutes

Nutrition Fact (per serving): 120 kcal (¼ oz. protein, 5½ oz. fat, 7 oz. of carbohydrates)

Ingredients (6 servings)

2 lbs. tomatoes

12 oz. paprika (green and red)

9 oz. cucumbers

1 ½ oz. onion

2 oz. white bread

½ cup tomato juice

½ fluid oz. olive oil, cold-pressed

1 pinch garlic powder

1 pinch salt and pepper

1 shot sherry vinegar

4 tablespoon water

Preparation

Slice the bread into small pieces and soak in the water for about 5 - 10 minutes. Then squeeze out the bread so that it loses the water. Peel the tomatoes, cut into 2 halves, and core. Also, cut the peppers in half and remove the seeds. Cut the cucumber into small pieces. Peel and then cut the onions it into small pieces.

In a bowl, put the vegetables with the garlic powder, salt, pepper, and the sherry vinegar and let everything marinate for about 7 minutes. Add the rest and mix everything well with the hand blender. You can add tomato juice if the soup is too thick, as needed. The soup should stay rather thick. Then chill the soup as it'll be eaten cold.

Salads

Canarian Potato Salad

Preparation time: 35 minutes

Cook time: 20 minutes

Nutrition fact (per serving): 222 kcal (¼ oz. protein, ½ oz. fat, 10¼ oz. of carbohydrates)

Ingredients (4 servings)

18 oz. small waxy potatoes

1 bunch parsley

1 lemon

1 clove of garlic

2 tablespoon whole almonds

2 oz. Cornichons (glass)

4 tablespoon olive oil

Salt and pepper to taste

Preparation

Thoroughly wash 18 oz. small waxy potatoes and cook with the skin in water for 19-22 minutes. Wash 1 bunch of parsley, shake dry, pull off the leaves, and chop finely. Wash 1 lemon with hot water, dry off, and finely grate the peel. Halve the fruit, squeeze one half. Peel 1 clove of garlic. Finely chop 2 tablespoon whole almonds (with skin), garlic, and 2 oz. cornichons (glass). Mix with parsley, lemon zest, lemon juice, and 4 tablespoons olive oil. Drain, rinse, and quarter the potatoes. Mix with the sauce and then season well with salt and pepper.

Chickpea and Sheep Cheese Salad

Preparation time: 15 minutes

Cook time: 30 minutes

Nutrition fact (per serving): 200 kcal (½ oz. protein, ½ oz. fat, 10 oz. of carbohydrates)

Ingredients (6 servings)

2 cans chickpeas

2 untreated lemons

1 bunch parsley

5¼ oz. sheep cheese

5 tablespoon oil

Salt, pepper and sugar to taste

Preparation

Add the chickpeas in a colander, rinse, and drain. Wash the lemons with hot water, rub dry and rub off the peel. Halve and squeeze the lemons. Wash the parsley, pat dry, pluck the leaves from the stalks, and roughly chop. Dice the sheep's cheese, mix with the chickpeas, parsley, 5 tablespoons lemon juice, lemon zest and oil, season with salt, pepper and sugar. Next, marinate for 29-33 minutes, and then season again.

Spanish Salad

Preparation time: 30 minutes

Nutrition fact (per serving): 252 kcal (½ ounce protein, 1 ounce of fat, ¼ ounce of carbohydrates

Ingredients (4 servings)

4 ripe tomatoes

10 ½ oz. cherry tomatoes

1 Chorizo sausage

1 onion

1 clove of garlic

½ bunch flat-leaf parsley

1 teaspoon and 4 tablespoon olive oil

5 tablespoon white wine vinegar

½ teaspoon mustard

Salt, pepper, and sugar to taste

3 oz. Spanish sheep cheese (Manchego)

Preparation

Wash tomatoes and rub dry. Quarter the cherry tomatoes and roughly dice tomatoes. Peel the chorizo and cut into thick slices. Peel and finely dice the onion and garlic. Wash the parsley and shake dry. Put 1 handle aside. Pluck the leaves from the remaining stems and chop finely. Heat 1 teaspoon of oil in a pan, fry the Chorizo in it for about 4 minutes until crispy. Remove and drain on kitchen paper. Mix the tomatoes, garlic, shallot, and chorizo in a bowl. Mix vinegar and mustard, season with salt, pepper, and sugar. Beat in 4 tablespoons of oil. Slice the cheese or use a peeler to cut into slices. Mix the vinaigrette and tomato mixture, season with salt and pepper. Finally, fold in cheese and then garnish with parsley.

Spanish Pork Chops with Avocado and Tomato Salad

Preparation time: 75 minutes

Cook time: 25 minutes

Nutrition fact (per serving): 833 kcal (2 oz. protein, 40 oz. fat, 40¼ oz. of carbohydrates)

Ingredients (4 servings)

1 big orange

1 garlic clove

Juice of 3 limes

½ cups and 3 tablespoon good olive oil

4 pork chops (approximately 7 oz. each)

3 oz. white bread (1–2 days old)

2 lbs. of potatoes

22 oz. tomatoes

1 onion

2 tablespoon butter

1 tablespoon white balsamic vinegar

1 ripe avocado

1 cup of milk

Salt, pepper, ground cumin, sugar

Preparation

Preheat the oven (electric stove: 350 ° F / convection: 300 ° F). For the sauce, peel the orange so that the white skin is completely removed. Cut the orange into pieces. Peel the garlic. Puree both with lime juice and ½ cup oil with a hand blender to a creamy sauce. Season to taste with salt, pepper, and 1 teaspoon of cumin.

Wash the chops, pat dry, cut in half, and pat a little flat. Place in a large baking dish or drip pan (deep baking tray). Crumble the bread and sprinkle it on the meat. Pour sauce over it. Braise in a hot oven for about 1 hour. In the meantime, peel, wash, and cut the potatoes into pieces. Cover and cook in salted water for 19-22 minutes.

Wash the tomatoes and cut them into large pieces. Skin the onion and cut into thin rings. Mix the vinegar with salt, pepper, and a pinch of sugar. Beat in 3 tablespoons of oil. Halve and pit the avocado. Remove the pulp from the skin and cut it into thin slices. Mix the tomatoes, onions, avocado, and vinaigrette together. Drain the potatoes for the puree. Add milk and butter and then mash into a puree. Season to taste with salt. Serve the chops with mashed potatoes and salad. Stir the sauce well again and serve.

Carrot Salad

Preparation time: 30 minutes

Cook time: 60 minutes

Nutrition fact (per serving): 250 kcal (1 ounce protein, 10 ounces fat, 5 ounces of carbohydrates)

Ingredients (4 servings)

2 oranges

18 ounces carrots

2 garlic cloves

3 tablespoons sherry vinegar

1 pinch salt

4 tablespoons olive oil

1 tablespoon chopped oregano

1 pinch white pepper

1 pinch ground cumin

½ teaspoon paprika powder

1 onion

2 tablespoons pine nuts

Preparation

Wash the untreated orange with hot water, pat dry, and rub the peel off. Squeeze both oranges. Put the orange juice with the grated zest in a saucepan. Wash, peel, and finely slice the carrots. Bring the orange juice with the skin to a boil, add the carrots, and cook covered over medium heat for about 10 minutes until al dente.

In the meantime, peel and finely chop the garlic and onion. Mix the vinegar with salt, mix with the olive oil, garlic, and spices. Drain the carrots and mix them with the sauce while still warm. Let the salad stand for about 1 hour. Roast the pine nuts in a pan without fat, and then sprinkle them over the salad.

Spanish Potato Salad

Preparation time: 75 minutes

Nutrition fact (per serving): 572 kcal (20 ¼ oz. protein, 30 oz. fat, 40 oz. of carbohydrates)

Ingredients (4 servings)

16 raw frozen prawns

3 lbs. potatoes

Salt and pepper to taste

1 red and yellow pepper

4 stem basil, thyme and oregano

4 garlic cloves

7 oz. mayonnaise for salad

7 oz. whole milk yogurt

1 tablespoon lemon juice

1 tablespoon oil

½ bunch arugula or rocket

4 wooden skewers

Preparation

Thaw prawns first and then peel and wash the potatoes. Boil in salted water for 22 minutes. Wash the peppers, cut into eighths, and remove the seeds. Place the pulp on a baking sheet. Grill under the grill for 10-12 minutes until the skin turns black and blisters. Remove and cover with a damp cloth until the pods have cooled. Wash the herbs, shake dry and cut into small pieces. Peel the garlic. Finely dice 2 toes. Mix together the mayonnaise and yogurt, season with salt, pepper, and lemon juice.

Stir in the garlic and herbs. Drain water from the potatoes and allow it to cool a bit. Peel off the skin of the peppers and cut the pulp into pieces. In the meantime, peel the prawns and remove the intestines. Wash the prawns, pat dry, and season with salt and pepper. Cut 2 cloves of garlic into slices. Heat the oil in a pan. Fry the prawns and garlic for 3-4 minutes, turning, and then remove.

Clean the rocket or arugula and cut it a little smaller. Cut the potatoes into wedges. Mix the potatoes, bell pepper, rocket/arugula, and aioli in a bowl. Put the prawns on 4 skewers and serve with the potato salad.

Spanish Lemon and Potato Salad

Preparation time: 60 minutes

Nutrition fact (per serving): 358 kcal (¼ ounce protein, 20 oz. fat, 1 ounce of carbohydrates)

Ingredients (4 servings)

2 lbs. waxy potatoes

Untreated lemon

3 white wine vinegar

5 tablespoon sunflower oil

1 lemon

1 head of radicchio salad

1 pink pepper berry

6 stems parsley

1 avocado

Sugar and salt to taste

Preparation

Wash the potatoes clean and boil it in salted water for 22-26 minutes. Drain, rinse, and peel the potatoes. Wash the lemon, rub dry and rub the peel. Halve and squeeze the lemon. For the vinaigrette, mix 4 tablespoons of lemon juice and vinegar, beat in the oil. Season the vinaigrette with a little sugar, salt, and lemon pepper. Cut the boiled potatoes into slices, mix with the vinaigrette, and leave to stand for about 2 hours. Clean, wash, and drain the radicchio. Pluck the leaves into bite-sized pieces. Wash the parsley, pat dry and roughly chop the leaves. Split the avocado in half, remove the core and peel, or remove from the peel with a tablespoon. Cut the avocado halves into slices. Season the potato salad again with salt and lemon pepper and fold in the radicchio, parsley, and avocado before serving.

Summer Melon Salad

Preparation time: 20 minutes

Nutrition fact (per serving): 157 kcal (1 oz. protein, 5 oz. fat, 2 oz. of carbohydrates)

Ingredients (4 servings)

1 watermelon

1 melon

6 tablespoon icing sugar

1/5 cup Maraschino liqueur

1 cup yogurt

3 tablespoons lemon juice

Preparation

Peel the watermelon, remove the seeds, and cut out small balls from the pulp with a spherical cutter. Do the same with the melon. Mix the melon ball well and put it in the fridge with 4 tablespoon of icing sugar and Maraschino for 1 hour. Fill the mixed melon balls into dessert glasses and set aside. Stir the yogurt with the lemon juice and 2 tablespoon of icing sugar and pour it over the melon balls.

Main Dishes and Appetizers

Spanish Braised Steaks

Preparation time: 60 minutes

Cook time: 90 minutes

Nutrition fact (per serving): 672 kcal (¼ oz. protein, 1 oz. fat, 1 ounce of carbohydrates

Ingredients (4 servings)

4 thick steaks (approximately 7 oz. each)

1 onion

1 clove of garlic

2 bell peppers

9 oz. cherry tomatoes

Salt and pepper to taste

1 tablespoon flour

2 tablespoons of oil

1 cup red wine

2 lbs. potatoes

3½ oz. green olives without pits

6 tablespoon olive oil

Preparation

Take steaks out of the refrigerator about 2 hours before frying. Peel and roughly dice onion and garlic. Clean, wash and dice the peppers. Wash tomatoes. Pat the meat dry. Season with salt and pepper and turn in flour. Coat a cast-iron pan with a little oil and heat it up. Fry the steaks in it for about 2 minutes on each side. Spread the steaks in a baking dish.

Heat 2 tablespoons of oil in the pan. Briefly sauté the onion, garlic and vegetables—season with salt and pepper. Deglaze with wine and 1 cup of water. Next, bring to the boil and simmer for about 2 minutes. Spread the vegetables on the steaks and stew in a hot oven (electric stove: 350 ° F / convection: 300 ° F) for about 2 hours.

Peel and wash the potatoes and cook in salted water for 19-22 minutes. Finely chop the olives. Drain the potatoes, collecting 1 cup of the cooking water. Add 6 tablespoons of olive oil to the potatoes and roughly mash everything. Stir in the olives. Season to taste with salt and serve.

Chorizo in Sherry and Pimentos De Padron

Preparation time: 10 minutes

Cook time: 15 minutes

Nutrition fact (per serving): 222 kcal (10 oz. protein, 1 oz. fat, 1 oz. of carbohydrates)

Ingredients (8 servings)

2 rings of Chorizo sausage (Spanish paprika sausage)

2 small onions

2 garlic cloves

1 bunch thyme

3 bay leaves

½ white dry sherry

Preparation

Cut the Chorizo into approximately ½ inches thick slices. Peel the onions and finely dice them. Peel garlic and chop finely. Wash the thyme, shake dry, and pluck the leaves from the stems. Fry the Chorizo in a large pan without fat for about 6 minutes or until crispy. Add onions, garlic and bay leaves, fry for another 4 minutes. Deglaze with sherry and 2 ½ fluid oz. water. Add the thyme, except for something to garnish. Bring to a boil and simmer for about 5-6 minutes or until the liquid has evaporated. Arrange the Chorizo in a bowl and garnish with the rest of the thyme leaves.

Chicken with Garlic

Preparation time: 20 minutes

Cook time: 60 minutes

Nutrition fact (per serving): 560 kcal (12 ounces protein, 5 ounces fat, 3 ounces of carbohydrates)

Ingredients (4 servings)

5 garlic cloves

1 teaspoon salt

5 tablespoons olive oil

1 pinch black pepper

18 ounces chicken pieces

1 tablespoon parsley chopped, smooth

Preparation

Peel and roughly chop the garlic, sprinkle with salt, and mash into a paste with a flat knife or a mortar. Put the paste in a bowl, add 2 tablespoons of olive oil and pepper, and mix everything into a marinade. Brush the chicken pieces with it and cover and marinate in the refrigerator for about 2 hours.

Heat the remaining olive oil in a pan, fry the chicken pieces vigorously, and fry them over medium heat for about 10 minutes until golden brown. Drain the meat on kitchen paper, sprinkle with the parsley, and serve.

Traditional Baked Meat and Vegetables

Preparation time: 30 minutes

Cook time: 120 minutes

Nutrition fact (per serving): 490 kcal (15 ounces protein, 3 ounces fat, 7 ounces of carbohydrates)

Ingredients (4 servings)

¾ cup olive oil

2½ cups Brandy

2 pounds chicken leg discs

3 Beefsteak tomatoes

1 vegetable onion, large

2 green peppers

2 medium eggplants

1 tablespoons olive oil

1 teaspoon sweet paprika powder

2 red peppers

1 zucchini

1 pinch salt and pepper

Preparation

Remove fat and tendons from the meat and cut into large pieces. Remove the tough skin from the eggplant and zucchini. Brush the peppers and peel the onion. Cut the vegetables into bite-sized pieces and cut the tomatoes into 2/3 inch thick slices. Cut the onion into eight pieces and peel it apart. Spread 1 tablespoon of olive oil on a flat, oven-safe dish. Place the meat cubes in the dish, season with salt and pepper, and sprinkle with paprika powder. Place the vegetables on the meat and cover with the tomato slices. Add salt and pepper.

Drizzle with a small glass of brandy and 1 glass of olive oil. Preheat the oven to 400 F and put the form in for 25 minutes. Then switch back to 340 F and cook for another 2 1/2 hours. When the tomato slices begin to brown, stir once quite thoroughly. The dish can also stew a little longer in the oven.

Pickled Camembert

Preparation time: 15 minutes

Nutrition fact (per serving): 250 kcal (2 ounces protein, 5 ounces fat, 2 ounces of carbohydrates)

Ingredients (4 servings)

6 branch marjoram

2 garlic cloves

1 tablespoon pickled green pepper

4 ½ ounces Camembert

1 teaspoon sunflower oil

1 Apple

Preparation

Wash the marjoram and pat dry well. Peel the garlic and cut into thin slices crosswise. Drain the green pepper well. Cut the Camembert into eighths and layer them alternately with marjoram, garlic, bay leaves, and green pepper in a sealable container. Top up with sunflower oil until the oil covers all ingredients. Close the jar tightly and let it steep for 2 days at room temperature. Wash and quarter the apple and cut out the core. Cut the quarters into wedges, carefully fold into the pickled Camembert and serve with hearty farmer's bread.

Mallorca Chicken and Almond Soup

Preparation time: 20 minutes

Cook time: 90 minutes

Nutrition fact (per serving): 450 kcal (20 ounces protein, 5 ounces fat, 8 ounces of carbohydrates)

Ingredients (6 servings)

2 carrots

½ celery bulb

½ leek

2 onions

2 garlic cloves

4 tomatoes (dried)

2 chicken breasts

7 ounces bacon

1 pinch salt

1 pinch pepper

4 shot dark bread

2 tablespoons oil

7 ounces grated almonds

Preparation

Wash the carrots, celery, and leeks well and cut away all inedible parts. Cut everything with peeled onions and cloves of garlic. Remove the tomatoes from the oil and cut it into strips. Put the bacon and meat in a stockpot, add all the vegetables, and cover about 2 liters of water. The broth is boiled once with two teaspoons of salt and then simmered over low heat for half hours.

In the meantime, de-crust the bread and cut it into cubes. Then roast them in oil in a pan, turning several times, until golden brown on all sides. Season with salt and pepper and drain on kitchen paper.

After the cooking time, the meat and bacon come out of the broth to cool, and the soup is pureed with the hand blender. Bring to a boil together with the added almonds. Cut away the notch from the bacon and then cut it into cubes with the chicken. Put both back in the soup, season it again, and serve sprinkled with the bread croutons.

Spanish Rabbit Pot

Preparation time: 40 minutes

Cook time: 80 minutes

Nutrition fact (per serving): 840 kcal

Ingredients (4 servings)

1 rabbit (approximately 4 lbs.)

5 ½ oz. black olives

4 red and green peppers (from the jar)

7 oz. shallots

1 garlic clove

4 tablespoon oil

1 tablespoon lemon juice

1 thyme

1 ¼ cups red wine

Rosemary stem

Sage leaves

Salt and pepper to taste

Bay leaves

Sugar to taste

Preparation

Wash the meat and cut off the abdominal flap. Cut the rabbit into approximately 8 parts. Drain the olives and peppers. Peel the shallots and garlic. Heat the oil and fry the meat and belly flaps. Season with salt and pepper. Remove the meat and keep warm. Steam the shallots and garlic in the frying fat. Stir in the thyme, rosemary, sage, and bay leaves. Deglaze with stock and wine, reduce a little. Add meat, pepperoni, and olives. Let simmer in the oven preheated on 390 °for about 100 minutes, before serving.

Meatballs in Date and Tomato Sauce

Preparation time: 30 minutes

Cook time: 30 minutes

Nutrition fact (per serving): 491 kcal (20 oz. protein, 20 oz. fat, 20 oz. of carbohydrates)

Ingredients (4 servings)

2 onions

1 clove of garlic

14 oz. mixed minced meat

1 egg

4 tablespoons breadcrumbs

2 oz. pitted dried dates

1 tablespoon oil

1 cups of dry red wine

1 can chunky tomatoes

1 tablespoon flour

Salt and pepper to taste

Nutmeg to taste

Red pepper flakes to taste

Preparation

Peel and finely dice 2 onions and 1 clove of garlic. Knead 14 oz. minced meat, 1 egg, 4 tablespoons breadcrumbs, garlic, and half of the onions. Season with salt, pepper, and nutmeg. Shape 16 balls out of it. For the sauce, finely dice 2 oz. pitted, dried dates. Clean, wash, and finely dice 1 red pepper. Heat 1 tablespoon of oil. Sauté the paprika and the rest of the onion in it. Add the dates, deglaze with 1 cup dry red wine. Add 1 can of chunky tomatoes, bring to the boil and season with salt and pepper. Turn the meatballs in 2 tablespoons of flour and add to the sauce. Then cook covered for about 24 minutes. Flip the balls once in between.

Chili Lemon Olives

Preparation time: 10 minutes

Nutrition fact (per serving): 111 kcal (¼ oz. protein, 10 oz. fat, ¼ oz. of carbohydrates)

Ingredients (4 servings)

3 stems of oregano

1 lemon

2 dried chili peppers

2 tablespoon olive oil

1 ½ cups pitted green olives

Preparation

Wash 3 stalks of oregano, shake dry, and remove the leaves. Wash the lemon with hot water, dry it, and finely grate the peel. Halve it, squeeze one half. Finely chop 2 dried chili peppers. 1½ cups pitted green olives. Mix with oregano, lemon zest, lemon juice, chili, and 2 tablespoons of olive oil.

Sherry Mushrooms

Preparation time: 45 minutes

Cook time: 20 minutes

Nutrition fact (per serving): 161 kcal (¼ ounce protein, ¼ ounce fat, ¼ ounce of carbohydrates)

Ingredients (4 servings)

22 oz. small mushrooms

3 garlic cloves

2 shallots

4 tablespoon olive oil

¾ cup dry sherry

6 stems parsley

Salt and pepper to taste

Preparation

Clean the mushrooms and wash if necessary. Peel 3 cloves of garlic and 2 shallots. Slice the garlic and cut the shallots into strips. Gradually heat 4 tablespoons of olive oil in a large pan. Fry the mushrooms vigorously in portions. Season with salt and pepper. Finally, fry the garlic and shallots briefly. Add all the mushrooms again, deglaze with ¾ cup dry sherry. Boil and simmer for 9-11 minutes. Wash 6 stalks of parsley, shake dry, pluck the leaves off, roughly chop, and stir.

White Beans with Chorizo

Preparation time: 20 minutes

Cook time: 20 minutes

Nutrition fact (per serving): 178 kcal (¼ oz. protein, 10 oz. fat, ½ oz. of carbohydrates)

Ingredients (4 servings)

1 onion

3½ oz. Chorizo (Spanish paprika sausage)

1 tablespoon olive oil

2 tablespoon tomato paste

1 can (2¼ cups) giant white beans

Salt and cayenne pepper to taste

Preparation

Peel and finely dice 1 onion. Peel off the skin of 3½ oz. Chorizo and dice the sausage. Heat 1 tablespoon olive oil. Fry the onion and chorizo in it for about 3 minutes. Stir in 2 tablespoons of tomato paste, deglaze with 1 cup of water, and boil. Pour 1 can white giant beans into a colander, rinse, drain, and add to the sauce. Simmer for 4-6 minutes. Season well with salt and cayenne pepper.

Oven Tomatoes

Preparation time: 35 minutes

Cook time: 20 minutes

Nutrition fact (per serving): 241 kcal (½ oz. protein, 10¼ oz. fat, ¼ oz. of carbohydrates)

Ingredients (4 servings)

6 tomatoes

2 oz. Spanish goat cheese

2 branches of rosemary

1 clove of garlic

5 tablespoon olive oil

5 tablespoon breadcrumbs

Salt and pepper to taste

Preparation

Preheat the oven (electric stove: 390 ° F/ convection: 350° F). Wash 6 tomatoes, cut in half, and place on a baking sheet with the cut surfaces facing up. Season with salt and pepper. Roughly grate 2 oz. of cheese. Wash 2 sprigs of rosemary, pat dry, pluck needles, and chop. Peel and chop 1 clove of garlic. Mix the cheese, rosemary, garlic, and 5 tablespoon breadcrumbs and spread on the tomatoes. Drizzle with 5 tablespoons of olive oil. Bake in the oven for 16–22 minutes and serve.

Marinated Zucchini

Preparation time: 25 minutes

Cook time: 20 minutes

Nutrition fact (per serving): 143 kcal (¼ oz. protein, 10 oz. fat, ¼ oz. of carbohydrates)

Ingredients (4 servings)

1 parchment paper

1 large zucchini

2 tablespoon olive oil

1 egg

5 stems of basil

2 tablespoon capers

2 tablespoon Lemon juice

Salt and pepper to taste

Preparation

Preheat the oven (electric stove: 390 ° F/ convection: 350 ° F). Line a baking sheet with baking paper. Clean and wash 1 large zucchini and cut into approximately 2 inches thick slices. Spread on the baking sheet. Season with salt and pepper, drizzle with 2 tablespoons of olive oil. Bake in the oven for about 10 minutes. Boil 1 egg hard for 10 minutes. Wash 5 basil stalks, shake dry, and pick off the leaves. Finely chop 2 tablespoon capers and basil. Quench the egg, peel, and dice. Mix 2 tablespoon lemon juice, 2 tablespoon olive oil, basil, and capers, fold in the egg. Serve the zucchini, top with the egg and caper mix.

Shrimp Pan with Parsley, Lemon, and Garlic

Preparation time: 25 minutes

Cook time: 20 minutes

Nutrition fact (per serving): 182 kcal (1 oz. protein, ¼ oz. fat)

Ingredients (4 servings)

28 oz. raw shrimp (1 oz. each; headless, in shell)

4 garlic cloves

1 untreated lemon

2 tablespoon olive oil

1 bunch parsley

Salt and pepper to taste

Preparation

Wash the shrimp and pat dry. Peel and slice the garlic. Wash lemon with hot water, rub dry, and cut into slices. Heat oil in a pan. Fry the shrimp for 7-9 minutes while turning. After 3 minutes, add the garlic and lemon and fry. Wash the parsley, shake dry, pluck the leaves from the stalks and roughly chop. Season the shrimp with salt and pepper. Add parsley and stir in. Serve with toasted bread.

Catalan Tortilla

Preparation time: 35 minutes

Cook time: 50 minutes

Nutrition fact (per serving): 444 kcal (10 oz. protein, 20 oz. fat, 30 oz. of carbohydrates)

Ingredients (4 servings)

2 lbs. waxy potatoes

2 (approximately 14 oz.) red peppers

1 onion

1 clove of garlic

5 tablespoon olive oil

5 eggs

½ cup of milk

3 stems of flat-leaf parsley

2 oz. grated Manchego cheese

Salt and pepper to taste

Preparation

Wash the potatoes thoroughly and cook covered in plenty of boiling water for 21-23 minutes. Rinse the potatoes under cold water, drain, and remove the peel. Cool the potatoes for approximately 3 hours and let them rest. Clean and wash the peppers and cut them into small cubes. Peel the onions and garlic. Finely dice the onion, press the garlic through a garlic press. Slice the potatoes. Heat 1 tablespoon of oil in a non-adhesive pan (1 inch diameter), sauté paprika, onion, and garlic in it for 4-6 minutes. Season with salt and pepper and remove. Put 4 tablespoons of oil in the hot pan and fry the potatoes for about 5 minutes while turning. Season with pepper and salt and fold in the paprika and onion mixture. Whisk the eggs, milk, cheese, approximately ½ teaspoon salt and a little pepper. Pour eggs, cheese, and milk over the potato and pepper mixture. Cover and let stand for 11-16 minutes over low heat. Let the tortilla slide onto a large, flat lid or plate. Return to the pan with the browned side up and fry for another 6 minutes. Wash the parsley, shake dry, and cut the leaves into strips. Arrange the tortilla on a large plate and cut into pieces like cake. Sprinkle with parsley.

Clam Pot with Chorizo

Preparation time: 25 minutes

Cook time: 20 minutes

Nutrition fact (per serving): 402 kcal (1 oz. protein, 10 oz. fat, 20 oz. of carbohydrates)

Ingredients (4 servings)

4 lbs. mussels

2 cups vegetable broth

6 tablespoon ketchup

1 ¼cups white wine

1 bunch spring onions

3 oz. Chorizo sausage

9 oz. cherry tomatoes

8 stems basil

8 stalks coriander

2 tablespoon olive oil

2 splash of Tabasco

Salt and pepper to taste

Preparation

Wash and clean the mussels. Sort out the open mussels. In a large saucepan, bring the broth, ketchup, and wine to the boil. Put the mussels in the saucepan and cook, covered, for 9-11 minutes, stirring occasionally. In the meantime, clean and wash the spring onions and cut into pieces approximately 1 inch in size. Dice the sausage. Wash tomatoes, drain, and cut in half. Wash the vegetables, shake dry, and finely chop except for a few basil leaves for garnish.

Heat the oil in a pot. Fry the sausage in it, turning, for about 4 minutes. Add spring onions and tomatoes after approximately 2 minutes. Remove the mussels from the broth. Sort out unopened mussels. Pour the cooking liquid using a sieve to the sausage. Add the chopped herbs and mussels again and stir in. Season to taste with salt, pepper, and Tabasco.

Spanish Prawns with Garlic and Olives

Preparation time: 180 minutes

Cook time: 30 minutes

Nutrition Fact (per servings): 270 kcal (20 oz. protein, 1 ounce of fat, ¼ oz. of carbohydrates)

Ingredients (4 servings)

2 garlic cloves

1/2 untreated lemon

3 stems fresh thyme

16 headless king prawns

2 Bay leaves

2 oz. each of green and black olives

½ cup olive oil

Red chili pepper

Salt

Preparation

Peel the garlic and cut into thin slices. Wash the chili, cut lengthways, core, and cut into fine rings. Cut the lemon into wedges. Wash and rinse the thyme, pat dry, and finely chop the leaves. Remove the shrimp from the shell and remove the intestines. Wash shrimp and pat dry well. Put the garlic, chili, thyme, bay leaf, lemon, and prawns in a bowl. Pour olive oil over it and leave to stand for about 2 hours. Drain the prawns and collect the marinade. Heat a small amount oil in a pan and fry the prawns for 5-6 minutes while turning. Finally, add the garlic and chili and fry briefly. Season with salt and place in a bowl with the olives. Serve garnished with lemon wedges and bay leaves.

Andalusian Mini Meatballs (Albondigas)

Preparation time: 40 minutes

Cook time: 20 minutes

Nutrition fact (per serving): 831 kcal (50 oz. protein, 40 oz. fat, 50 oz. of carbohydrates)

Ingredients (4 servings)

½ bunch parsley

2 discs toast

2 garlic cloves

3 onions

25 oz. ground beef

1 teaspoon ground cumin

1 teaspoon ground coriander

2 eggs

7 oz. long grain rice

5 tablespoons oil

2 tablespoon tomato paste

2 cans chunky tomatoes

1 teaspoon sugar

3 tablespoons of dry sherry

1 oz. butter

1 knife point ground saffron or turmeric

Salt and pepper to taste

Preparation

Wash the parsley, shake dry, pluck the leaves from the stems, and chop. Put something aside to sprinkle. Soak toast in cold water. Peel the garlic and 1 onion and dice very finely. Knead the 1½ teaspoons of salt, 1 teaspoon of pepper, mince, parsley, diced onion, garlic, cumin, coriander, eggs and pressed bread. Shape approximately 20 meatballs from the minced meat with damp hands.

Prepare the rice in boiling salted water according to the instructions on the packet. Heat 3 tablespoons of oil in a large pan, fry the meatballs in it, turning over a medium heat for 7-9 minutes and then remove. In the meantime, peel and finely chop 2 onions. In a fry pan heat up 2 tablespoons of oil, sauté onions, add tomato paste, sauté briefly, pour in tomatoes. Season with salt, pepper and a little sugar. Cover and simmer over medium heat for 9-11 minutes. Pour in the sherry, season to taste again. Add meatballs, heat briefly. Drain the rice in a colander and drain. Put the pot back on the stove and melt the butter in it. Add saffron, sweat briefly, add rice, and hen mix. Arrange everything, sprinkle with parsley.

Madrid Meatballs in Tomato Sauce

Preparation time: 35 minutes

Cook time: 20 minutes

Nutrition fact (per serving): 452 kcal (30 oz. protein, 20 oz. fat, ½ oz. of carbohydrates)

Ingredients (4 servings)

2 onions

1 clove of garlic

18 oz. ground beef

1 egg

4 tablespoons of breadcrumbs

4 tablespoons of milk

2 tablespoons of tomato paste

½ teaspoon Sambal Oelek

1 pinch ground cumin

1 pinch ground coriander

3 tablespoons of olive oil

18 oz. ripe tomatoes

1 tablespoon of dry sherry

1 pinch sugar

Little freshly ground nutmeg

Salt and Chili pepper to taste

Small bunch of parsley

Preparation

Peel the garlic and onions and cut into fine cubes. Wash parsley and shake dry. Except for something to garnish, pluck the leaves from the stems and chop. Knead the mince, half of the onions, garlic, egg, breadcrumbs, milk, parsley, and 1 tablespoon tomato paste. Season with salt, Sambal Oelek, 1 pinch of cumin, coriander, and a little nutmeg. Shape into 24 meatballs. Heat 2 tablespoons of oil in a frying pan and fry the meatballs all around for 6-9 minutes. Clean and dice the tomatoes. Heat 1 tablespoon of oil and steam the onions until translucent while turning. Stir in 1 tablespoon tomato paste, add tomatoes, and sherry. Wash and clean and cut the chill into fine rings. Bring the tomatoes to the boil and season with salt, chili and sugar. Simmer the sauce for 6-9 minutes and arrange the sauce and balls in clay bowls then garnish with parsley.

Squid in Tomato and Garlic Sauce

Preparation time: 30 minutes

Cook time: 30 minutes

Nutrition fact (per serving): 113 kcal (1/5 oz. protein, 1/5 oz. fat, 1/10 oz. of carbohydrates)

Ingredients (6 servings)

4 squid tubes

1 onion

1 clove of garlic

1 tablespoon oil

1 can tomatoes

½ cup of vegetable broth

2 teaspoons capers

Salt and pepper to taste

Sugar to taste

Preparation

Split the squid tubes in half horizontally and cut into pieces. Peel onion and garlic and chop finely. Heat the oil in a pot. Fry the squids in it, turning, for about 3 minutes. Put onion and garlic and fry for 2 minutes and season with salt and pepper. Deglaze with tomatoes and vegetable stock. Chop the tomatoes a little with the spatula. Cover and simmer for about 42-46 minutes. Add the capers 10 minutes before the end of the cooking time and cook. Season to taste with pepper, salt and sugar, let cool down a little, and serve.

Paella Pans

Preparation time: 45 minutes

Cook time: 30 minutes

Nutrition fact (per serving): 450 kcal

Ingredients (12 servings)

9 oz. pre-cooked frozen shrimp (without heads and shells)

11 oz. frozen mussels

21 oz. chicken fillet

2 lbs. Chorizo (Spanish paprika sausage)

2 red peppers

1 vegetable onion

2 garlic cloves

2 tomatoes

2 tablespoons of olive oil

14 oz. paella or risotto rice

2 teaspoons Pimentón de la Vera dulce

4 cups hot chicken broth

2 jars saffron threads

3 ½ oz. frozen peas

3 ½ oz. mayonnaise

Parsley to taste

Preparation

Thaw the prawns and mussels in a colander, rinse with cold water and drain. Rinse the chicken with cold water, pat dry and cut into small cubes. Cut the Chorizo into slices. Clean and wash the peppers and cut into small cubes. Peel the onion and chop finely. Peel the garlic and chop finely. Wash, quarter and core the tomatoes and cut into small cubes. Heat the oil in a large (paella) pan. Fry the chicken and Chorizo in it, turning, for about 3 minutes, remove. Sauté the bell pepper, onion and garlic in the frying fat for 3 minutes. Add rice and diced tomatoes, dust with Pimentón. Mix the hot broth with the saffron, pour in, bring to the boil and cook for 11–16 minutes on a low heat. Add the chicken, chorizo, mussels, prawns, and frozen peas. Next, mix everything well. Cover and cook for 11-14 minutes. Mix the mayonnaise with the rest of the garlic, a little salt, and pepper. Sprinkle the paella with parsley. Add the garlic sauce.

Spanish Braised Steaks

Preparation time: 35 minutes

Cook time: 60 minutes

Nutrition fact (per serving): 672 kcal (2 oz. protein, 1 oz. fat, 1 ½ oz. of carbohydrates)

Ingredients (4 servings)

4 thick hoof steaks

1 onion

1 clove of garlic

1 bell pepper

9 oz. cherry tomatoes

2 tablespoon flour

7 tablespoons of oil

1 cup red wine

2.2 lbs. potatoes

3 1/2 oz. green olives without pits

6 tablespoon olive oil

Salt and pepper

Preparation

Take steaks out of the refrigerator about 2 hours before frying. Peel and roughly dice onion and garlic. Clean, wash, and dice the peppers. Wash tomatoes. Pat the meat dry. Season with salt and pepper and turn in flour. Coat a cast-iron pan with a little oil and heat it up. Fry the steaks in it for about 3 minutes on each side. Spread the steaks in a baking dish.

Heat 2 tablespoons of oil in the pan. Briefly sauté the onion, garlic and vegetables. Season with salt and pepper. Deglaze with wine and 1 cup of water, bring to the boil, and simmer for about 3 minutes. Spread the vegetables on the steaks and stew in a hot oven heated to 350 F for about 2 hours.

Peel and wash the potatoes. Next, a cook in salted water for 18-21 minutes. Finely chop the olives. Drain the potatoes and keep 1 cup of the cooking water. Add 6 tablespoons of olive oil to the potatoes and roughly mash everything. Stir in the olives. Season to taste with salt and serve.

Spanish Chicken Schnitzel with Yellow Rice and Onions

Preparation time: 35 minutes

Cook time: 30 minutes

Nutrition fact (per serving): 811 kcal (50 oz. protein, 30 oz. fat, 50 oz. of carbohydrates)

Ingredients (4 servings)

1 onion

3 garlic cloves

7 tablespoons oil

1 teaspoon sugar

1 1/2 tablespoon tomato paste

1 can tomatoes

¾ cup vegetable broth

1 freshly ground black pepper

1 sweet paprika

4 tablespoon dry sherry

2 oz. almonds (skinless)

4 chicken fillets

5 1/2 oz. Creme fraiche Cheese

7 oz. basmati rice

1 large bunch of spring onions

10 saffron thread

Salt to taste

Preparation

Peel the onion and garlic and chop finely. Heat 2 tablespoons of oil in a fry pan. Fry the onion in it, turning. Finally, add the garlic and fry. Sprinkle with sugar and caramelize. Add the tomato paste, sweat briefly, deglaze with tomatoes and stock. Season with salt, pepper and paprika. Bring to a boil and simmer over low to medium heat for 6–8 minutes. Season to taste with sherry.

In the meantime, roughly chop the almonds. Wash the meat, pat dry and cut in half horizontally, so that two flat edges are formed. Heat 3 tablespoons of oil in a large pan. Fry the meat in portions on each side for about 2 minutes. Season with salt and pepper.

Put the tomato sauce in a large flat or small baking dish, spread the schnitzel on top. Spread crème fraîche evenly on top and bake in the preheated oven (electric stove: 390 ° F/ convection: 350 ° F) for 12–15 minutes. At the same time, prepare the rice in boiling salted water according to the instructions on the package. Cook the almonds and saffron with the rice right from the start. Clean and wash the spring onions, remove some of the spring onion greens, and cut into fine rings. Heat 2 tablespoons of oil in a large pan, fry the spring onions in it, turning them all over. Sprinkle the baked schnitzel with pepper and spring onion greens and serve with spring onions. Add saffron and almond rice in a bowl.

Königsberger Klopse Spanish Style

Preparation time: 30 minutes

Cook time: 30 minutes

Nutrition fact (per serving): 654 kcal (30 oz. protein, 40 oz. fat, 10 oz. of carbohydrates)

Ingredients (4 servings)

Bread roll from the day before

1 onion

1 anchovy

3 oz. skinless almond kernels

18 oz. mixed minced meat

1 egg

1/2 teaspoon medium-hot mustard

1/2 red and yellow pepper

1 oz. butter or margarine

1 oz. flour

3 1/2 oz. black Kalamata olives

1 packet saffron threads

¾ cups milk

Few squirts of lemon juice

Salt and pepper to taste

Preparation

Soak the rolls in cold water. Peel the onions and cut them small. Finely chop the anchovy. Grill the almonds in a frying pan without oil. Take them out, let them cool a bit, and roughly chop. Set aside 2 tablespoons of chopped almonds. Knead the mince, anchovies, the squeezed bun, onion, remaining almonds and egg. Season with ½ teaspoon salt, pepper and mustard. Shape approximately 12 dumplings with moistened hands.

Bring lightly salted water to the boil. Add the dumplings and let simmer for 10–12 minutes over a low heat. Clean and wash the peppers and cut into small cubes. Take out the dumplings. Pour the stock through a fine sieve and measure out 2 ½ cups.

Melt the fat in a saucepan. Add the flour and saffron threads and sweat in them. Add in the broth and milk, stirring constantly, and simmer for 4-6 minutes over low heat, stirring occasionally. Wash the parsley, shake dry, and cut into thin strips. Season the sauce with salt, pepper, and lemon juice. Add the dumplings and olives to the sauce. Arrange the dumplings on plates and sprinkle with parsley strips, diced paprika, and chopped almonds.

Spanish Chicken Pan

Preparation time: 20 minutes

Cook time: 20 minutes

Nutrition fact (per serving): 432 kcal (1 ½ oz. protein, 20 oz. fat, ½ oz. of carbohydrates)

Ingredients (4 servings)

4 onions

2 garlic cloves

6 beefsteak tomatoes

4 chicken fillets

3 tablespoon olive oil

2 oz. almond kernels

1 ¼ cups dry white wine

Salt and pepper to taste

1/2 bunch flat-leaf parsley

3 1/2 oz. black olives (without pits)

Preparation

Peel and finely dice onions and garlic. Wash tomatoes, roughly dice. Wash the meat, pat dry. Warm up the oven (electric stove: 350 ° F / convection: 300 ° F). Heat oil in a pan and fry the fillets on each side for 4-5 minutes. Place in an ovenproof dish and finish cooking in the hot oven for 9-11 minutes.

Briefly toast the almonds in the frying fat. Sauté the onions, garlic, and tomatoes. Deglaze with wine and season with salt and pepper. Simmer for 6–8 minutes. Wash and roughly chop parsley. Add to the vegetables with olives.

Murcia Meatballs

Preparation time: 25 minutes

Cook time: 35 minutes

Nutritional Fact (per serving): 272 kcal (1/2 oz. protein, 1/6 oz. fat, 1/5 oz. of carbohydrates)

Ingredients (5 servings)

6 stems of parsley

2 onions

2 garlic cloves

10 ½ oz. ground beef

1 egg yolk

1 oz. breadcrumbs

2 tablespoons of oil

1 ripe tomato

1 ½ lemons

2 tablespoon of olive oil

Salt and pepper to taste

Small chili pepper

Preparation

Wash the parsley, shake dry, pluck the leaves off, and chop finely. Peel and finely dice the onions and 1 clove of garlic. Peel the second clove of garlic and cut into thin slices. Wash, clean and thinly slice the chili pepper. Mix the mince, egg yolk, breadcrumbs, half of the onion cubes, garlic cubes, and chili. Season with salt and pepper. Shape the mixture into small balls. Add the oil in a pan, heat up, and fry the balls for 5–8 minutes, turning.

Wash, clean, quarter, and core the tomatoes. Cut the pulp into small cubes. Heat olive oil in a saucepan and sauté the garlic slices in it. Add the rest of the onion cubes, tomatoes and lemon juice and simmer for 4-6 minutes. Put the meatballs and simmer for another 5 minutes. Season to taste with salt and pepper. Sprinkle with parsley.

Spanish Bean Pot

Preparation time: 20 minutes

Cook time: 35 minutes

Nutrition fact (per serving): 493 kcal (20 oz. protein, 20 ½ oz. fat, 1 oz. of carbohydrates)

Ingredients (4 servings)

22 oz. colorful peppers

½ perennial celery stalk

32 oz. ripe tomatoes

1 onion

¼ oz. garlic clove

1 small sprig of rosemary

1 ring chorizo sausage

2 tablespoon olive oil

1 rose peppers

1 teaspoon dried oregano

2 cups vegetable broth (instant)

2 cans white beans

Salt and pepper to taste

Preparation

Clean and wash the peppers and celery and cut into large pieces. Wash the tomatoes, pat dry, and roughly dice. Peel the onion and garlic. Cut the onion into large cubes, chop the garlic. Wash the rosemary and pat dry. Cut the sausage into thick slices. Heat the oil in a saucepan, fry the sausage, and briefly fry the onion and garlic. Stir in paprika, celery, and tomatoes and season with salt, pepper, rose paprika and oregano. Add the rosemary, pour in the stock, and bring to the boil. Cover and braise for 25-30 minutes. Put the beans on a sieve, drain them, and after 22-24 minutes, add them to the pan. Season the finished bean pot again with salt and pepper and arrange in a bowl or a terrine.

Spanish Potato Casserole

Preparation time: 25 minutes

Cook time: 75 minutes

Nutrition fact (per serving): 641 kcal (40½ oz. protein, 30½ oz. fat, 20 oz. of carbohydrates)

Ingredients (4 servings)

18 oz. pork goulash

2 onions

3 tablespoons of oil

1/3 cup dry white wine

18 oz. potatoes

1 zucchini

1 oz. butter or margarine

1 oz. flour

2 oz. grated Manchego cheese

1 cup milk

1 cup clear broth (instant)

1 egg yolk

5 ½ oz. Chorizo sausage

Salt and pepper to taste

Preparation

Pat the meat dry. Peel and dice the onions. Heat 1 tablespoon of oil in a roaster. Fry the meat in it. Add onions and fry briefly. Season with salt and pepper. Deglaze with wine and 1 cups of water and cook for 42-46 minutes. Peel, wash, and slice the potatoes. Heat 2 tablespoons of oil in a pan. Fry the potatoes in it, turning, for 9-12 minutes or until golden brown. Clean, wash, and slice the zucchini. Add to the potatoes 5 minutes before the end of the roasting time. Season with salt and pepper and set aside.

Heat the fat in a saucepan and sweat the flour in it. Deglaze with milk and stock while stirring. Season to taste with salt and pepper. Mix the egg yolks and some sauce and stir into the sauce. Cut the sausage into slices. Mix the potatoes, zucchini, sausage, and meat. Put everything in a baking dish. Spread the sauce over it. Pour cheese over it and bake in an oven preheated to 350 ° F for 9-12 minutes, before serving.

Spanish Potato Pan with Chorizo

Preparation time: 20 minutes

Cook time: 40 minutes

Nutrition fact (per serving): 492 kcal (10½ oz. protein, 1 oz. fat, 1½ oz. of carbohydrates)

Ingredients (4 servings)

3 lbs. potatoes

9 oz. Chorizo (Spanish paprika sausage)

1 red chili pepper

8 shallots or small onions

3 tablespoons of oil

1 bunch chives

Salt and pepper to taste

Preparation

Cover and cook the potatoes in water for 18-22 minutes. In the meantime, peel off the skin of the sausage, cut the sausage into slices. Clean the chili, score lengthways, remove the seeds, wash and cut into fine rings. Peel the shallots and cut in half or into quarters depending on the size. Rinse the potatoes in cold water, peel them and let them cool down a little. Slice the potatoes. Heat the oil in a very large pan or two. Fry the sausage slices until crispy while turning and remove. Fry the potatoes in the hot frying fat for 11 minutes until golden brown. After 5 minutes add the shallots and chili, continue frying. Fold in the sausage and heat briefly. Wash the chives, pat dry, and cut into fine rolls. Season the fried potatoes with salt and pepper.

Spanish Potato Mince Tortilla

Preparation time: 75 minutes

Cook time: 50 minutes

Nutrition fact (per serving): 540 kcal (30 oz. protein, 1½ oz. fat, 1 oz. of carbohydrates)

Ingredients (4 servings)

4 ½ lbs. potatoes

5½ oz. mushrooms

2 handles sage

1 onion

8 eggs

5 tablespoon olive oil

2/3 lb. minced meat

1 teaspoon tomato paste

2 oz. pitted green olives

Salt and pepper

Preparation

Cover the potatoes and cook them in water for 16–18 minutes. Drain, quench, and peel. Allow to cool slightly. Clean the mushrooms, wash them if necessary, and cut them in half. Wash the sage, pat dry, chop the leaves. Peel the onion and cut into strips. Whisk the eggs, season with salt and pepper. Heat 2 tablespoons of oil in a big non-stick pan with a lid. Fry the minced meat in it until crumbly and remove. Fry the mushrooms and sage in the hot frying fat. Take out and mix with mince and tomato paste. Season with salt and pepper to taste.

Dice the potatoes. Heat 3 tablespoons of oil in the frying fat. Fry the potatoes in it. Fry the onion briefly. Season with salt and pepper. Spread the olives and minced meat on top. Pour the eggs on top. Cover everything and let stand for 22-26 minutes over low heat.

Spanish Tapas

Preparation time: 20 minutes

Cook time: 30 minutes

Nutrition fact (per serving): 351 kcal (30 oz. protein, 10 ½ oz. fat, ½ oz. of carbohydrates)

Ingredients (4 servings)

9 oz. spinach leaves

9 oz. minced meat

2 eggs

5 tablespoons of breadcrumbs

Pepper and sweet paprika

5½ oz. hard cheese (e.g., Spanish Manchego cheese)

8 cherry tomatoes

2 cups flour

10 tablespoons of oil

1 Rosemary and thyme

Preparation

Clean and wash the spinach. Put in a little boiling salted water and let it collapse and cool down a little. Squeeze out well and chop roughly. Knead the mince with the spinach, 1 egg, 1 tablespoon breadcrumbs, salt, pepper, and paprika. Shape into 8 balls.

Cut the cheese into 16 pieces. Wash the tomatoes and cut into 16 slices. Whisk 1 egg. Turn the cheese one after the other in the flour, egg, and the rest of the breadcrumbs. Turn tomatoes in flour and knock them off lightly. Place 2 pieces of cheese and tomato slices alternately on skewers.

Heat the oil in a large pan. Fry the mince balls and the cheese skewers one after the other for 7-11 minutes or until golden brown. Drain well on kitchen paper. Arrange everything and garnish if necessary. Olives and fresh white bread pair well with this.

Braised Rabbit the Spanish Way

Preparation time: 40 minutes

Cook time: 95 minutes

Nutrition fact (per serving): 880 kcal (2½ oz. protein, 1½ oz. fat)

Ingredients (5 servings)

10½ oz. carrots

2 onions

2 garlic cloves

2 sprigs of rosemary

6 stems thyme

9 oz. Chorizo sausage

1 ready-to-cook rabbit

1 teaspoon of salt

4 tablespoon olive oil

2½ cups Rioja wine

2½ cups vegetable broth

10½ oz. cherry tomatoes

3 juniper berries

2 bay leaves

7 oz. prunes

1 can of chickpeas

½ bunch parsley

4 stems basil

Preparation

Peel the carrots, onions, and garlic and cut into cubes. Wash the rosemary and thyme, shake dry. Peel off the sausage skin. Cut the sausage into slices. Divide the rabbit into 7-8 pieces, wash and pat dry, and season with salt. Heat the oil in a roasting pan. Fry the sausage slices until crispy while turning, remove. Fry the rabbit parts vigorously all around in the hot fat. Add onions, carrots, garlic, rosemary, and thyme and fry briefly. Deglaze with wine and broth and bring to the boil. Wash the tomatoes. Place the juniper, bay leaves, tomatoes, sausage and prunes in the roaster. Braise in a preheated oven (electric stove: 390 ° F/ convection: 350 F) for about 2 hours. Add the chickpeas 20 minutes before the end of the cooking time. Wash the parsley and basil, shake dry and pluck the leaves from the stems and cut into strips. Arrange the rabbit with the sauce in a large bowl and sprinkle with the prepared herbs.

Spanish Mussel Noodle

Preparation time: 20 minutes

Cook time: 30 minutes

Nutrition fact (per serving): 870 kcal (30 oz. protein, 30 oz. fat, 80 oz. of carbohydrates)

Ingredients (4 servings)

2 lbs. mussels

2 onions

3 garlic cloves

4 tablespoons of oil

1 cup dry white wine

14 oz. noodles (e.g. croissant noodles)

7 oz. Bratchorizo sausage

1 oz. grated Parmesan cheese

1 can chunky tomatoes

1 oz. butter

2 tablespoons of tomato paste

2 tablespoons lemon juice

Salt and pepper to taste

Preparation

Clean and wash the mussels thoroughly. Carefully place any open mussels on a work surface. If they don't close or move, throw them away. Peel, half, and cut the onions into strips. Peel and slice the garlic. Heat 3 tablespoons of oil in a saucepan, fry the onions and garlic in them until translucent. Season with salt and pepper. Pour white wine and 3 cups water, bring to the boil. Add the mussels and cook, covered, over medium heat for about 8 minutes. Pour the mussels onto a sieve and collect the stock. Throw away any unopened mussels.

Prepare the pasta in boiling salted water according to the instructions on the packet. Remove the sausage from the skin and cut into slices. Remove the mussel meat from the shell, except for 10–12 pieces. Brush a pan with 1 teaspoon of oil. Fry the sausage slices in it, turning them for 3-4 minutes, add tomatoes, butter, tomato paste and 1 ½ cups mussel stock, simmer for 4-5 minutes, fold in the whole mussels, pasta, and cheese. Season the pasta with salt, pepper and a little lemon juice.

Spanish Chicken Fillet With Bread and Pepper Sauce

Preparation time: 20 minutes

Cook time: 70 minutes

Nutrition fact (per serving): 738 kcal (40 oz. protein, 2 oz. fat, 20 oz. of carbohydrates)

Ingredients (4 servings)

18 oz. red peppers

15 tablespoons of oil

1 cup vegetable broth

3 oz. bulgur (coarse wheat groats)

11 oz. cherry tomatoes

3 bunches flat-leaf parsley

3 stems mint

2 shallots

3 tablespoons of lemon juice

Salt and pepper to taste

2 slices of toast

2 garlic cloves

3 oz. almond kernels with skin

¼ teaspoon hot and fiery chili flakes

1 pinch of sugar

4 chicken fillets

Preparation

Clean and wash the pepper. Pat dry. Heat 3 tablespoons of oil in a large pan, put the paprika in with the skin side in and fry vigorously. The skin should be light brown, but not burnt. Remove from the pan, drain on kitchen paper, and let cool. In the meantime, bring the vegetable stock to the boil. Add the bulgur, bring to the boil briefly and cover and simmer over low heat for 15–20 minutes. Clean, wash, and finely dice tomatoes.

Wash the parsley and mint, shake dry and pluck the leaves, except for 4 leaves for garnish, and cut into fine strips. Peel and finely dice shallots. Mix together lemon juice, salt, and pepper. Beat in 2 tablespoon olive oil. Mix the bulgur, shallots, parsley, mint, tomatoes, and vinaigrette. Let it steep for 30 minutes. Peel off the skin of the peppers. Peel the garlic and roughly chop the almonds.

Roughly crumble the toast. Put paprika, almonds, 8 tablespoons of olive oil, garlic, 5 tablespoons of water, and chili in a tall mixing bowl. Puree with a hand blender. Season to taste with salt, pepper, and sugar. Wash the meat, pat dry. Heat 2 tablespoons of oil in a pan and fry the meat over medium heat for about 12 minutes, turning. Season with salt and pepper. Remove from pan and cut open. Arrange the meat and parsley salad on plates.

Spanish Pepper Noodle Pan

Preparation time: 10 minutes

Cook time: 30 minutes

Nutrition fact (per serving): 570 kcal (30 oz. protein, 28 oz. fat, 33 oz. of carbohydrates)

Ingredients (5 servings)

18 oz. thrown pork neck (piece)

7 oz. Cabanossi

22 oz. tomatoes

3 bell peppers

1 onion

1 garlic clove

1 tablespoon Almond kernels (skinless)

2 tablespoons oil

9 oz. spaghettini

½ bunch of basil

Salt and pepper to taste

Preparation

Pat the meat dry and roughly dice. Cut the cabanossi into slices. Clean, wash and chop tomatoes and peppers. Peel and thinly dice the onion and garlic. If necessary, roughly chop the almonds. Heat the oil in a large stew pan. Fry the meat vigorously all around. Fry the Cabanossi briefly. Sauté the onion, garlic, paprika, and almonds for about 3 minutes. Spice up. Add tomatoes and ¾ cups water, simmer for 11-13 minutes. Break the pasta into pieces. Pour into the pan, stir in. Simmer for another 10 minutes. Stir every now and then, possibly adding some more hot water. Season the pasta pan to taste. Wash and pluck the basil, sprinkle over it.

Spanish Garlic Rabbit (Conejo De Ajo)

Preparation time: 15 minutes

Cook time: 60 minutes

Ingredients (4 servings)

3 1/3 lbs. ready-to-cook rabbit

4 tablespoons olive oil

18 oz. tomatoes

4 garlic cloves

1 red pepper

6 onions

3/4 cups pepper-stuffed olives

½ fluid oz. white wine

Salt and white pepper to taste

Preparation

Divide the rabbit into 8 portions, season. Heat the oil in a roasting pan. Fry the rabbit thoroughly on all sides. Score the tomatoes crosswise, scald, peel, and dice. Peel and chop the garlic. Clean and wash the peppers and cut them into strips. Peel and quarter the onions. Braise everything in the frying fat while stirring. Add olives and wine, bring to the boil. Add pieces of rabbit. Cook everything in a hot oven (electric stove: 390 ° F/ convection: 350 ° F) for 42-46 minutes.

Spanish Potato Tortilla

Preparation time: 10 minutes

Cook time: 50 minutes

Nutrition fact (per serving): 310 kcal (½ oz. protein, 10 oz. fat, 20½ oz. of carbohydrates)

Ingredients (2 servings)

22 oz. waxy potatoes

2 bell peppers

1 clove of garlic

1 tablespoon olive oil

1 egg

½ cup of milk

Chili powder or sweet paprika

3 stems parsley

Salt and pepper to taste

Chili pepper to taste

Preparation

Wash the potatoes and cook for about 15 minutes. Quench, peel and let cool. Clean and wash the peppers and cut into rings or strips. Peel and finely chop the garlic. Cut the potatoes into slices that are not too thin. Heat the oil in a coated pan (approximately 1-inch diameter; with lid). Fry the potatoes for 4-6 minutes, turning them occasionally. Add paprika and garlic and fry for 5-6 minutes. Season with salt and pepper. Whisk eggs and milk together. Season well with salt, pepper, and chili. Pour over the potatoes and cover and let stand for 15-20 minutes over low heat. Use a flat lid to turn and fry briefly. Wash the parsley, cut into strips and sprinkle on top.

Spanish Asparagus Tortilla

Preparation time: 20 minutes

Cook time: 40 minutes

Nutrition fact (per serving): 394 kcal (30 oz. protein, 1 ounce of fat, ½ oz. of carbohydrates)

Ingredients (4 servings)

2 lbs. white asparagus

3 spring onions

8 eggs

½ fluid ounce milk

3 ½ oz. Serrano ham, thinly sliced

2 tablespoon oil

Grated nutmeg

Salt and white pepper to taste

Chervil and lettuce leaves

Preparation

Peel and wash and the asparagus and chop off the woody ends. Cut the asparagus into pieces. Clean and wash the spring onions and cut into thick rings. Whisk eggs and milk together. Season well with salt, pepper, and nutmeg. Heat 1 tablespoon oil in a coated pan (approximately 4 inches in diameter; with lid). Add half asparagus in it. Fry for 5-6 minutes until fully cooked. Fry half the spring onions briefly. Pour half of the egg-milk over it. Cover and let stand for 11-16 minutes over low heat. Turn the tortilla with the lid or a plate and fry for another 2-4 minutes. Keep warm. Rub the pan with kitchen paper. Heat 1 tablespoon of oil. Bake a second tortilla using leftover asparagus, spring onions, and egg-milk. Top the tortillas with ham.

Spanish Artichoke Pot

Preparation time: 25 minutes

Cook time: 45 minutes

Nutrition fact (per serving): 381 kcal (10 oz. protein, ½ oz. of fat, 60 oz. of carbohydrates)

Ingredients (4 servings)

3 lbs. small potatoes

3 tablespoons of oil

2 cans of artichoke hearts

5 medium-sized tomatoes

6 small onions

4 stems parsley

1 bay leaf

½ cups of white wine

Salt and white pepper to taste

Preparation

Peel and wash the potatoes and cut in halves or quarters. Heat the oil in a large pan. Fry the potatoes in it for 21-26 minutes, turning occasionally. Drain the artichoke hearts from the tin, cut in half lengthways. Peel off the skin. Cut the tomatoes into small pieces. Peel, halve, or quarter the onions. Wash and pluck the parsley and cut into fine strips. After 15 minutes, add the onions, tomatoes, and bay leaves to the potatoes and fry them. Add the artichokes, deglaze with wine. Cover and simmer for about 5 minutes. Season with salt, pepper, and cloves. Sprinkle with parsley.

Spanish Asparagus Plate

Preparation time: 20 minutes

Cook time: 40 minutes

Nutrition fact (per serving): 322 kcal (½ oz. protein, 1 oz. fat, ¼ oz. of carbohydrates)

Ingredients (5 servings)

2 lbs. white asparagus

2 teaspoons of lemon juice

1 egg

1 teaspoon medium-hot mustard

1 tablespoon white wine vinegar

¾ fluid ounce oil

13 oz. skimmed milk yogurt

1 garlic clove

1 rosemary and basil

1 onion

1 beefsteak tomato

4 peppercorns

12 oz. Spanish Serrano ham

Stalk thyme

Caper apples or capers

Preparation

Wash and peel the asparagus. Cut off woody ends. Boil the asparagus lightly salted water with 1 teaspoon of sugar and lemon juice for 18-20 minutes. Mix the egg, salt, mustard, and vinegar with the cutting stick. Beat the oil drop by drop. Stir in the yogurt. Season to taste. Peel the garlic. Wash herbs shake dry. Chop everything and stir under 1/3 of mayonnaise. Peel and chop the onion. Wash, clean, core and finely dice tomatoes. Crush peppercorns. Stir everything into the 2/3 of mayonnaise. Lift out the asparagus and let it cool. Wrap with ham. Serve with the mayonnaise. Garnish with basil, lemon, and caper apples. Baguette or farmhouse bread goes well with it.

Spanish-Style Asparagus with Two Kinds of Sauces

Preparation time: 15 minutes

Cook time: 30 minutes

Nutrition fact (per serving): 910 kcal (10 oz. protein, 80 ½ oz. fat, 10 oz. of carbohydrates)

Ingredients (4 servings)

4 1/2 lbs. white asparagus

1 teaspoon sugar

¼ oz. butter or margarine

1 egg

1 teaspoon fine medium-hot mustard

1 tablespoon lemon juice

1 cup sunflower oil

Grated zest of 1 untreated lemon

2 cups roasted paprika

1 medium onion

4 tablespoon sherry vinegar or white wine vinegar

Pepper to taste

5 tablespoons of olive oil

8 thick chives

7 oz. Serrano ham in thin slices

1 lemon

Salt

Preparation

Wash and peel the asparagus, cut off the woody ends. Add the asparagus in plenty of boiling salted water. Add a pinch of sugar and fat and cook for 15-20 minutes, depending on the thickness. In the meantime, for the mayonnaise, place the egg, mustard, remaining sugar, ½ teaspoon salt and lemon juice in a tall mixing bowl.

Mix well with the whisk of the hand mixer or a cutting stick. Then gradually pour in the oil while stirring. Stir 2/3 of the lemon zest into the finished mayonnaise and season with salt and pepper. Put in a cool place. Drain the peppers and dice very finely. Skin the onion and cut into fine cubes. Mix the vinegar, salt, pepper, and onion together and fold in the olive oil.

Stir in the diced paprika. Lift the asparagus out of the water, drain well and let cool down a little. Wash the chives, briefly add them to the hot asparagus water and immediately place them in cold water. Divide the asparagus into 8 portions and tie together with a stalk of chives.

Arrange 2 asparagus packets per person with a little sauce, mayonnaise, and ham on plates or small platters. Serve garnished with lemon and sprinkled. Add the remaining paprika sauce and mayonnaise.

Spanish Baked Redfish

Preparation time: 20 minutes

Cook time: 40 minutes

Nutrition fact (per serving): 374 kcal

Ingredients (4 servings)

1 small, ready-to-cook redfish (about 3 lbs.)

Untreated lemon

Slices of toast

1 garlic clove

1 bunch parsley

1 tablespoon Sweet paprika

6 tablespoons oil

1 teaspoon salt

Olives

Preparation

Rinse the fish inside and out with cold water and dry. Cut 4 wedges from the lemon, squeeze the rest and sprinkle the fish with them. Debark and crumble bread. Peel and finely chop the garlic. Wash the parsley, put a stalk in the fish belly, and chop the rest. Mix the bread, garlic, parsley, and paprika together. Spread 2 tablespoons of oil in a roasting pan. Season the redfish inside and outside with salt, put in. Replace the upper eye with olives if you like. Make four 1/3 inch deep incisions in the fish and insert lemon wedges. Spread the bread-spice mixture over it, drizzle with the remaining oil. Bake in an oven preheated to 390 ° F for 35-45 minutes.

Seville Meatballs

Preparation time: 30 minutes

Cook time: 30 minutes

Nutrition fact (per serving): 520 kcal (1 oz. protein, 30 oz. fat, 10¼ oz. of carbohydrates)

Ingredients (4 servings)

Bread roll from the day before

1 cup milk

1 onion

1 garlic clove

11 oz. tomatoes

1 stems marjoram

3 tablespoon olive oil

1 tablespoon flour

1 cup vegetable broth (instant)

7 tablespoons dry sherry

18 oz. mixed minced meat

1 egg

Salt and pepper to taste

Handles flat-leaf parsley

Olives

Preparation

Soak the rolls in the milk. Peel and finely dice onions. Peel the garlic, press with a garlic press. Clean, wash, and diced tomatoes. Wash and chop marjoram. Heat 1 tablespoon of olive oil. Sauté 2 onions and 2 cloves of garlic in it. Dust with flour. Deglaze with the stock and 5 tablespoons of sherry. Add the tomatoes and season with salt, pepper, and marjoram. Let simmer for 14-16 minutes. In the meantime, squeeze out the rolls. Knead with the mince, remaining onion and garlic, egg, and 2 tablespoons sherry. Season with salt and pepper. Shape it into small balls with floured hands. Heat 2 tablespoons of olive oil. Fry the balls all around for about 5 minutes. Then add to the sauce and finish cooking for another 5 minutes. Wash the parsley, cut into fine strips, and sprinkle over the sauce. Season again to taste and serve garnished in portions with olives and fresh marjoram.

Spanish Paella

Preparation time: 20 minutes

Cook time: 40 minutes

Nutrition fact (per serving): 570 kcal (40½ oz. protein, 10½ oz. fat, 60 oz. of carbohydrates)

Ingredients (4 servings)

1 onion

1 garlic clove

1 red, green, and yellow pepper

5½ oz. frozen peas

8 chicken drumsticks

1 tablespoon olive oil

9 oz. risotto rice

1 can ground saffron

5 ½ cups chicken broth (instant)

8 headless prawns in shell

1 lemon

Salt and pepper to taste

Preparation

Peel onion and garlic and chop finely. Split the peppers in half, remove the seeds, wash, pat dry and cut into bite-sized pieces. Thaw the peas. Wash the chicken drumsticks and pat dry. Heat the oil in a large saucepan. Fry the chicken legs in it, turning all over until golden brown. Season with salt and pepper. Remove and set aside. Put the onion in the frying fat and sauté until translucent.

Add garlic and paprika and fry. Add risotto and fry with it. Add the saffron, deglaze with the stock. Bring to the boil, place the chicken legs next to each other and cover and simmer over medium heat for about 35 minutes. In the meantime, wash the prawns and peel them except for the tail fin. Remove bowel and 12 minutes before the end of the cooking time, mix in the peas, and place the shrimp side by side on the rice dish. Wash the lemon, rub dry, cut into slices and serve.

Spanish Potatoes

Preparation time: 15 minutes

Cook time: 20 minutes

Nutrition fact (per serving): 430 kcal (10 oz. protein, 1 ounce of fat, 40 oz. of carbohydrates)

Ingredients (4 servings)

2 lbs. of potatoes

1 red and green pepper

1 onion

1 garlic clove

1 teaspoon cumin

3 tablespoons of olive oil

12 slices Serrano ham

2 teaspoons of sweet paprika

2 tablespoons of sherry vinegar

Salt and chili pepper to taste

Parsley

Preparation

Wash the potatoes and boil for 18-22 minutes. Clean and wash the peppers and cut them into cubes. Peel and dice the onion. Peel and roughly chop the garlic. Finely crush the garlic and cumin in a mortar. Stir in 2 tablespoons of oil, paprika, and vinegar. Season to taste with salt and chili. Drain, rinse, peel, and cut the potatoes. Heat 3 tablespoons of oil in a pan and fry the potatoes in it. Add the onion and bell pepper and fry for about 5 minutes. Add the garlic mixture to the potatoes. Season again with salt and pepper. Garnish the potatoes with parsley and serve with ham.

Spanish Tortilla

Preparation time: 20 minutes

Cook time: 30 minutes

Nutrition fact (per serving): 452 kcal (10 oz. protein, 20 oz. fat, 30 oz. of carbohydrates)

Ingredients (4 servings)

2.2 lbs. waxy potatoes

6 tablespoon olive oil

9 oz. onions

2 garlic cloves

5 eggs

5 tablespoons whipped cream

2 tablespoons chopped parsley

Salt and pepper to taste

Preparation

Peel and clean the potatoes and slice into 2 inches thick. Heat four tablespoons of oil in a large pan. Fry the potato slices in portions until crispy brown. Put all the slices in the pan and continue frying for 9-11 minutes over medium heat. Peel and finely chop the onions and garlic. Add to the pan for the last 4-6 minutes and season with salt and pepper. Whisk eggs and cream, season with salt, pour over the potatoes. Cover and let stand for 16-20 minutes over low heat. Shake the pan from time to time, so that the tortilla doesn't stick to the bottom. Flip the tortilla onto a plate. Heat the remaining oil. Put the tortilla into the pan with the browned side up and fry for another 5-6 minutes. Arrange on a plate and serve sprinkled with the parsley.

Spanish Paella with Chicken Wings

Preparation time: 20 minutes

Cook time: 40 minutes

Nutrition fact (per serving): 465 kcal (1 oz. protein, 10 oz. fat, 1½ oz. of carbohydrates)

Ingredients (4 servings)

4 chicken wings

2 tablespoons of olive oil

1 medium onion

1 clove of garlic

7 oz. short grain rice

8 small prawns

1 cup white wine

1 cup chicken broth

1 bay leaf

1 sprig of rosemary

1 red pepper

1 zucchini

Saffron threads

Salt and pepper to taste

Preparation

Wash the chicken wings and season with salt and pepper. Heat the oil in a pan and fry the chicken wings in it for about 5 minutes. In the meantime, peel and finely dice the onion. Peel the garlic and cut into fine slices. Remove the chicken wings and set aside. Roast the garlic in the frying fat until golden. Add onion and sweat. Add rice and saffron, glaze briefly and top up with white wine and chicken stock. Add the chicken wings, bay leaves, and rosemary and simmer for 16-19 minutes.

In the meantime, wash and clean the peppers and zucchini. Cut the bell pepper into approximately 0.2 inches thick strips and the zucchini into approximately 0.12 inches thick slices.

Add the peppers and zucchini to the paella 12 minutes before the end of the cooking time. Peel and wash the prawns, remove the intestines and season with salt and pepper. Add the prawns to the paella about 2-3 minutes before the end of the cooking time. Season with pepper and salt and serve in the pan.

Spanish Meatballs in Tomato Sherry Sauce

Preparation time: 20 minutes

Cook time: 25 minutes

Nutrition fact (per serving): 893 kcal (50 oz. protein, 2 oz. fat, 1 oz. of carbohydrates)

Ingredients (4 servings)

2 onions

2 lbs. mixed minced meat

1 egg

1 tablespoon breadcrumbs

2 oz. Serrano ham

1 tablespoon oil

2.2 lbs. beefsteak tomatoes

1 garlic cloves

2 tablespoons of olive oil

2 tablespoon of tomato paste

1 bay leaf

1 tablespoon dry sherry

12 oz. quark (or cottage cheese, curd cheese)

3 oz. sheep's cheese

4 slices white bread

2 oz. arugula or rocket

Salt and pepper to taste

Sweet paprika

Preparation

Peel the onions. Place the mince in a bowl. Grate an onion. Add the egg and breadcrumbs and knead. Season to taste with salt, pepper, and paprika. Dice the ham very finely. Knead under the mince. Shape 12 small meatballs. Heat oil in a large pan. Fry the meatballs vigorously on both sides, remove. Place beefsteak tomatoes in boiling water, drain and rinse. Skin and dice the tomatoes. Peel the garlic. Finely dice 1 clove of garlic and remaining onion.

Heat 1 tablespoon of olive oil. Sauté the garlic and onion cubes in it. Add tomatoes, tomato paste, bay leaf, and sherry bring to the boil and reduce for 5-7 minutes. Season to taste with salt and pepper. Put the meatballs and sauce in a baking dish. In the preheated oven (electric stove: 390 ° F/ convection: 350 ° F) bake for about 14-16 minutes. Mix the quark. Crumble the sheep's cheese and stir in. Season to taste with salt and pepper. Arrange in a bowl and drizzle with 1 teaspoon of olive oil. Halve the bread slices if necessary. Finely chop the remaining clove of garlic. Heat 2 tablespoons of olive oil in a big pan. Add the garlic. Fry the bread slices in it until golden brown. Clean and wash the arugula. Take the casserole out of the oven and sprinkle with arugula.

Paella Valencia

Preparation time: 15 minutes

Cook time: 25 minutes

Nutrition fact (per serving): 393 kcal (9 oz. protein, 5 oz. fat, 30 oz. of carbohydrates)

Ingredients (4 Servings)

1 poularde

5 onions

2 garlic cloves

5 tomatoes

3 peppers

1 can of green peas

1 can of beans

18 oz. fish (turbot)

1 pinch of salt and pepper

1 pinch saffron

1 cube broth

7 oz. crab or crayfish

2 cups oil

2 cups of rice

Preparation

Heat 2 cups of oil very strongly in a hot pan. Make sure that you use a heat-resistant oil that does not burn. Cut a poularde into pieces, rinse thoroughly underwater, and pat dry. Fry vigorously all around in the hot fat. The meat should have typical roasting traces and aromas. Remove the pieces of chicken from the pan and set them aside.

Remove the flowers and seeds from three bell peppers, wash and cut into bite-sized pieces. Fry briefly in the remaining fat and add to the chicken. Skin 5 onions, cut in half, and cut into even rings. Caramelize in the pan. Wash 5 tomatoes, scratch the skin crosswise, and scald with hot water for half a minute. Skin the chicken with a knife and add the skinned tomatoes to the onions. Let the chicken pieces and diced paprika slide back into the pan.

Rinse two cups of rice under cold water, drain well, and add to the pan's contents. Pour 10 cups of vegetable or chicken broth. Peel and crush two cloves of garlic. Clean and wash 18 oz. fresh green beans and break one or two times, depending on the size. Alternatively, you can also use canned beans (drained weight 14 oz.). Add the garlic and beans to the rice. Season everything well with salt, pepper and paprika powder. Add a pinch of saffron. As soon as the rice has ingested the liquid, carry out the cooking test. If the rice is still very crunchy, add some broth. At the end of the cooking time, add a can of green peas.

Wash 18 oz. firm fish fillet, pat dry, drizzle with lemon juice, and lightly salt. Cut into large cubes. Add crab together with the turbot to the cooked rice and let it steep for 5-7 minutes. The finished Paella Valenciana is usually brought to the table in the pan.

Arroz Negro

Preparation time: 10 minutes

Cook time: 25 minutes

Nutrition fact (per serving): 561 kcal (20 oz. protein, 3 oz. fat, 29 oz. of carbohydrates)

Ingredients (2 Servings)

28 oz. calamari, medium-sized

2 green peppers

18 oz. paella rice

4 tablespoons olive oil cold pressed

1 pinch of salt

2 sachets of calamari ink

1 shot of fish stock in a ratio of 1: 3 to the rice volume

Preparation

Use a large pan for cooking the ingredients. The Spaniards use a special paella pan, which is made of cast iron and has a flat edge. Place some olive oil in the pan and heat it. Spread the calamari pieces in it and fry quickly on all sides. Add the pepper pieces and fry until the pulp begins to soften. Fold in rice and fry as well. The ingredients must be well mixed so that the taste can develop. Deglaze the ingredients with the fish stock and bring to the boil. For the final seasoning, sprinkle with paprika powder and season with salt. Finally, stir the calamari ink into the paella. Be careful with the amount, since the taste is strong! Over-seasoning can be avoided by adding the bags one at a time. Usually, the use of four bags is excessive.

Let the paella cook slowly and stop stirring. It has to simmer undisturbed over medium heat. The dish is ready when the rice is cooked, and most of the liquid has been used up. Bring down the pan from the cooking stove and let it rest for 4-6 minutes. Cover a pan with a fresh kitchen towel before serving.

Calamari in a Spicy Tomato Sauce

Preparation time: 20 minutes

Cook time: 55 minutes

Nutrition fact (per serving): 232 kcal (5 oz. protein, 4 oz. fat, 4 oz. of carbohydrates)

Ingredients (2 Servings)

18 oz. squid, only the tubes

14 oz. tomatoes, lumpy

2 tablespoons of tomato paste

2 medium-sized onions

2 garlic cloves

2 sprigs thyme

1 bay leaf

3 ½ oz. olives, black, pitted

2 tablespoons capers

1 chili pepper

1 pinch of salt and pepper

3 tablespoons olive oil

Preparation

Prepare the calamari by carefully washing the squid tubes and cutting them into rings about 1 inch thick. In the next step, cut the olives into small rings and chop the chili pepper, onions, and garlic cloves. Make sure that the garlic pieces aren't too small. Heat 3 tablespoons of olive oil in a pan and sweat the onion, garlic, and chili pieces. Now stir the tomato paste into the mixture and let it fry a little. Add the calamari rings in this stock and mix the whole thing carefully. Add the chunky tomatoes, the thyme sprigs, and the bay leaf. Season well with salt and pepper and let it simmer gently for at least 26 minutes with the lid closed. Stir every frequently; and if too much liquid evaporates, please add a little more water. Finally, roughly chop the capers and add them to the sauce with the olives. Let everything simmer again for about 11 to 16 minutes with the lid open. Lastly, season a little or add a dash of olive oil.

Panellets

Preparation time: 15 minutes

Cook time: 45minutes

Nutrition fact (per serving): 462 kcal (15 oz. protein, 2 oz. fat, 25 oz. of carbohydrates)

Ingredients (1 serving)

18 oz. almonds, blanched and ground

18 oz. sugar

16 oz. sweet potatoes

18 oz. pine nuts

1 egg yolk

1 lemon's grated peel

Preparation

Cook the sweet potatoes in a large saucepan with plenty of water for 33-36 minutes. The shell shouldn't be removed beforehand. After about 30 minutes, you should check the cooking condition with a knife. If the sweet potatoes' consistency is still too hard, the cooking time should be increased accordingly. Once they are soft, you can then drain the sweet potatoes and rinse them with cold water. This makes the subsequent peeling process easier. The peeled potatoes are now grated to a fine pulp with the grater in a large bowl. Alternatively, you can mash them with a fork.

Carefully mix ground almonds with the sugar and the grated lemon peel. When the ingredients are well mixed, they should be added to the grated sweet potatoes and kneaded into a homogeneous and even mass. This solid pulp is then rolled into small balls with a diameter of about 2 inches. You should be able to form around 45-60 balls from the pulp. The number of courses varies with the size of the balls. When the dough is processed, you can spread the pine nuts on a plate or board and roll the balls in them so that they are evenly covered. The pine nuts should be pressed down as firmly as possible so that the panels do not fall apart. Moisten the balls generously with the egg yolk to keep their shape, and the pine nuts get more hold. However, no egg should get into the clay itself, as the starch of the sweet potatoes gives them a sufficient binding agent.

Preheat oven to 360 ° F, and line a tray with baking paper on which the panellets can be placed. Depending on the size, these should now bake for about 6-8 minutes. Always keep an eye on the balls because they can get too hard very quickly. The ideal consistency has a crunchy skin and a creamy, fine melting core. The panellets taste particularly good warm, but can also be enjoyed cold.

Spanish Roulades

Preparation time: 20 minutes

Cook time: 95 minutes

Nutrition fact (per serving): 860 kcal (30 oz. protein, 3 oz. fat, 12 oz. of carbohydrates)

Ingredients (4 servings)

3 onions

3 cloves of garlic

1 red pepper

2 oz. green olives, stone-free

2 oz. almonds

4 beef roulades, approximately 8 oz. per piece

1 pinch of black pepper

1 pinch of salt

1 pinch of flour

2 tablespoons of oil

1 can of tomatoes

1 cup sherry, dry

Preparation

Peel and finely chop 3 onions and 3 cloves of garlic. Wash and quart 1 red pepper and then cut into small cubes. Chop 2 oz. seedless green olives and 2 oz. Place 4 beef roulades on the work surface and add pepper and salt. Generously spread almond and paprika topping are lavishly spread over it. Carefully roll up roulades and pinned with wooden skewers.

Carefully roll roulades in a little flour. Then put 2 tablespoons of oil in a pan and heat. When oil is hot enough, place the roulades in the pan and fry on all sides until they are lightly browned. Take roulades out of the pan and steam the chopped onions and the chopped garlic in the gravy for about 1 minute until they are translucent. Add the roulades again. Then add 1 can of pizza tomatoes and 1 cup of dry sherry to the pan and bring everything to a boil over high heat. Cover the roulades and braise over medium heat for about 100 minutes, turning them several times. When the cooking time is over, remove the roulades from the pan again. Season the sauce with pepper and salt. Finally, add the roulades to the sauce again.

Wheat Flour Tortillas

Preparation time: 20 min

Cook time: 30 minutes

Nutrition fact (per serving): 261 kcal (3½ oz. protein, 10½ oz. fat, 15½ oz. of carbohydrates)

Ingredients (12 servings)

26 ½ oz. flour smooth

1½ cup water

½ cup oil

1 teaspoon of salt

Preparation

Mix all the ingredients together and knead or mix until elastic dough has formed, add water or flour to achieve the right texture. Cover and let stand for at least half an hour. Divide the dough into 12 equal pieces and roll out thinly with a little flour. Heat a large non-stick pan and fry tortillas without fat on both sides until the dough bubbles. Leave tortillas soft, so they're easier to roll.

Spanish Canelones with Vegetables

Preparation time: 30 minutes

Cook time: 45 minutes

Nutrition fact (per serving): 250 kcal, (9½ oz. protein, 3½ oz. fat, 10 oz. of carbohydrates)

Ingredients (4 servings)

1 Melanzani

1 tablespoon of oil (for the pan)

7 oz. spinach

3 garlic cloves

1 teaspoon of ground cumin

3½ oz. mushrooms

10 canelones (cannelloni)

1 pinch of salt

1 pinch of pepper

2½ oz. Mozzarella cheese

Tomato sauce

1 tablespoon of olive oil

1 onion

2 garlic cloves

28 oz. canned tomatoes

1 teaspoon sugar

3 branch fresh basil

Preparation

Wash the eggplant and cut into small, bite-sized pieces. Then heat some oil in a pan and fry the pieces for 3-4 minutes over low heat. Peel and finely chop the garlic cloves. Clean the mushrooms well and cut them into slices. Then add the garlic, mushrooms, spinach and cumin to the pan with the eggplant pieces and fry for 3-4 minutes. Season to taste with salt and pepper. Pour the mixture into the already cooked canelones and place them next to each other in a greased baking dish. Preheat the oven to 370 ° F. Cut the tomatoes into small pieces, wash and finely chop the basil. Cut the mozzarella into slices. Peel the two cloves of garlic and the onion, finely chop and fry in hot oil for 3-4 minutes until translucent. Add the basil, tomatoes and sugar and let the sauce simmer for 6 minutes. Spread the sauce over the filled canelones, cover with the mozzarella slices, and bake for 28-32 minutes.

Chorizo Iberia

Preparation time: 20 minutes

Cook time: 30 minutes

Nutritional facts (per serving): 291 kcal (½ oz. protein, 20 oz. fat, ¼ oz. carbohydrates)

Ingredients (4 servings)

8 mini Chorizo picante

2 red onions

1 clove of garlic

1 stems thyme

1 bay leaf

1 cup dry red wine

Salt and pepper

Preparation

Halve the Chorizo lengthways. Peel the onions and cut into wedges. Peel and chop the garlic. Leave the Chorizo crispy in a pan without fat. Add the garlic and onions and sauté. Wash the thyme and shake dry. Add the thyme and bay leaves to the chorizo. Pour in the red wine and let it simmer halfway. Season with salt and pepper.

Three Basque Pintxos

Preparation time: 20 minutes

Cook time: 20 minutes

Nutritional facts (per serving): 560 kcal (10½ oz. protein, 30 oz. fat, 30 oz. of carbohydrates)

Ingredients (4 servings)

2 oz. walnut kernels

11 oz. goat cream cheese

2 garlic cloves

1 tablespoon mayonnaise

1 onion

1 tablespoon olive oil

1 teaspoon brown sugar

1 egg

1 teaspoon raspberry jam

2 Chorizo wurst

4 Pimientos de Padrón (fried peppers)

1 stem parsley

Salt and pepper

Baguette

Sliced Serrano ham

Preparation

Finely chop walnuts. Shape the cream cheese into 4 balls with cool hands and roll them in the walnuts. Refrigerate. For the aioli, peel and finely chop the garlic. Combine the mayonnaise and garlic, season with salt and pepper. Peel, halve and cut the onions into strips. Heat 1 tablespoon of oil in a frying pan. Fry the onions in the frying pan until it is brown. Scatter sugar on top and caramelize lightly. Take out the onion and let cool down a little. Heat 1 tablespoon of oil in the frying pan. Beat in the egg and season with salt. Fry for about 2 minutes on each side, remove and cut into 4 pieces.

Cut the Chorizo into slices. Wash the pimientos and pat dry well. Heat 1 tablespoon of oil in the frying pan. Fry the chorizo and pimientos for 4-5 minutes, turning. Remove from the heat and sprinkle the pimientos with sea salt. Wash the parsley and shake dry, chop the leaves. Cut the baguette into 12 slices. Cover 4 slices of baguette with Serrano ham, onion, and 1 piece of egg each. Divide 1 cream cheese ball and 1 teaspoon jam onto 4 more slices, sprinkle with parsley. Cover the remaining 4 bread slices with chorizo and pimientos and drizzle with a little aioli. Secure the topping with wooden skewers.

Chorizo Prawns "Pop 'N' Roll"

Preparation time: 10 minutes

Cook time: 35 minutes

Nutritional facts (per serving): 60 kcal (1½ oz. protein, 1 oz. of fat, ½ oz. of carbohydrates)

Ingredients (4 servings)

24 raw shrimp (fresh or frozen, without head and shell)

7 oz. Chorizo wurst

1 branch rosemary

½ cup of orange juice

2 tablespoon oil

Preparation

If necessary, let the shrimp thaw. Cut the Chorizo into 24 slices. Cut the shrimp lengthways on the back and remove the intestines. Wash the prawns and pat dry. Put the prawns and Chorizo slices on wooden skewers. Wash the rosemary, pat dry, strip the needles from the branches, chop finely and stir with the orange juice. Marinate the skewers for 28-32 minutes. Heat oil in a large pan. Pat the skewers dry and fry in portions for about 3 minutes on each side.

Gambas in Garlic Oil
(Gambas Al Ajillo)

Preparation time: 10 minutes

Cook time: 15 minutes

Nutrition fact (per serving): 242 kcal (40 oz. protein, ½ oz. fat, ½ oz. of carbohydrates)

Ingredients (4 servings)

20 frozen prawns

4 garlic cloves

Salt and pepper to taste

6 tablespoons of olive oil

Preparation

Thaw the prawns at room temperature. Peel the garlic and cut into thin layers. Peel the prawns, except for the tail fin, and remove the intestines. Wash the prawns and pat dry. Season with salt and pepper. Heat oil in a pan. Fry the prawns, turning, for approximately 5-8 minutes. Add the garlic and fry. Arrange in a bowl.

Manchego Balls with Paprika Salsa

Preparation time: 10 minutes

Cook time: 20 minutes

Nutrition fact (per serving): 373 kcal (1 oz. protein, 20 oz. fat, ½ oz. of carbohydrates)

Ingredients (6 servings)

2 red and yellow peppers

2 spring onions

1 tablespoon lemon juice

1 tablespoon olive oil

1 slice toast

2 tablespoon flour

1 egg

3 tablespoon whipping cream

14 oz. Manchego cheese

Salt and Pepper to taste

Preparation

Quarter the peppers, clean, wash, pat dry, and finely dice. Wash the spring onions, pat dry and cut into fine rings. Season the lemon juice with salt, pepper, and sugar. Beat in the oil drop by drop. Mix the peppers, spring onions, and vinaigrette together. Cut bread into pieces and grind in the universal chopper. Mix the flour and breadcrumbs. Stir the egg and 2 tablespoons of heavy cream, season with a little salt and pepper.

Dice Manchego cheese turn first in egg, then in the flour mixture, and press down. Heat the frying oil. Fry the cheese in portions until golden brown, remove, and allow to drain on kitchen paper. Arrange the paprika salsa and cheese on small plates.

Chorizo in Red Wine

Preparation time: 20 minutes

Cook time: 35 minutes

Nutrition fact (per serving): 340 kcal (10½ oz. protein, 1 oz. fat, ½ oz. of carbohydrates)

Ingredients (6 servings)

6 Chorizo sausages

5 stems sage

1 teaspoon oil

2 teaspoon honey

4 teaspoon dark balsamic vinegar

2 ½ fluid ounce of dry red wine

Preparation

Peel the sausage and cut into slices. Wash the sage, pat dry, pluck the leaves from the stems, and chop. Brush a coated pan with oil and heat. Fry the Chorizo in it, turning, for 3 minutes. In between, dab the fat out of the pan with a paper towel. Put honey in the pan and let it caramelize. Douse with balsamic vinegar and red wine, add sage, simmer for 2-3 minutes. Remove and let cool down, before serving.

Wrinkled Potatoes with Herb Sauce (Patatas Arugas Con Mojo Verde)

Preparation time: 20 minutes

Cook time: 45 minutes

Nutrition fact (per serving): 240 kcal (½ oz. protein, 10 oz. fat, 20 oz. of carbohydrates)

Ingredients (4 servings)

21 oz. small potatoes

18 1/2 oz. coarse sea salt

½ bunch parsley

10 stems coriander

2 garlic cloves

1 knife point ground cumin

1 tablespoon sherry vinegar

6 tablespoons of olive oil

Pepper to taste

Preparation

Wash the potatoes thoroughly with a brush. Spread 18 oz. salt and potatoes evenly on a baking sheet. Cook in a preheated oven (electric stove: 390 ° F/ convection: 350 ° F) for 35-43 minutes. In the meantime, wash the herbs, shake dry and pluck the leaves except for something to garnish from the stems and chop. Peel and slice the garlic. Mix the herbs, garlic, cumin, vinegar, and oil together. Season well with salt and pepper. Arrange the mojo verde in a bowl. Set up the potatoes on a platter and garnish with the remaining herbs.

Trio of Tapas

Preparation time: 20 minutes

Cook time: 20 minutes

Nutrition fact (per serving): 453 kcal (20¼ oz. protein, 30¼ oz. fat, 10¼ oz. of carbohydrates)

Ingredients (4 servings)

1 garlic clove

1 handle flat-leaf parsley

1 stem thyme

2 tablespoons of olive oil

9 oz. green olives (filled with almonds)

9 oz. black olives (with pits)

12 small mushrooms

12 cherry tomatoes

2 handles basil

1 tablespoon of oil

6 slices Serrano ham

2 figs

7 oz. Manchego cheese

2 teaspoon dried cranberries

Preparation

Peel garlic and chop finely. Wash the herbs, shake dry, and finely chop. Mix the olive oil, garlic and herbs. Roll green and black olives separately and fill into small bowls. Brush and clean mushrooms. Wash cherry tomatoes and rub dry. Wash the basil, shake dry, and pluck the leaves from the stems. Heat the oil and fry the mushrooms in a frying pan, take out, and let cool. Divide the ham slices in half and place 1 ham slice on each mushroom. Place a cherry tomato on each ham and pin it with a wooden skewer. Garnish with basil. Wash the figs, pat dry, and cut into 4 wedges. Cut the cheese into 8 cubes. Skewer 1 fig wedge on each cheese cube with a wooden skewer. Put a little cranberry on each fig. Arrange everything on a plate.

Spanish Remoulade

Preparation time: 15 minutes

Ingredients (2 servings)

1 egg yolk

2 teaspoon medium-hot mustard

1 tablespoon white wine vinegar

1 cup of sunflower oil

1 stems thyme, parsley and oregano

2 oz. roasted peppers

2 tablespoon pickled jalapeños

1 clove of garlic

1 teaspoon tomato paste

Sweet paprika

Salt, pepper, sugar to taste

Preparation

Take the egg and mustard out of the refrigerator at least 1 hour beforehand so that they're at the same temperature as the oil. Place a damp cloth under a wide bowl so that it stands securely. Mix the egg yolks, mustard, vinegar and a pinch of salt with a whisk until smooth. Add the oil drop by drop while stirring. As soon as about half of the oil has been stirred in, you can add it in a thin stream and mix it in. If your arm is getting heavy in the meantime, you can now swap the whisk for the hand mixer. Season the finished mayonnaise with salt, pepper and sugar and refrigerate. Wash the herbs and shake dry. Pluck the leaves and chop finely. Finely dice the peppers and jalapeños. Peel garlic and chop finely. Mix everything with tomato paste and mayonnaise. Season with salt, pepper, sweet paprika, and 1/2 teaspoon of sweet paprika. Chill the tartar sauce until serving.

Spanish Bruschetta

Preparation time: 15 minutes

Cook time: 15 minutes

Nutrition fact (per serving): 252 kcal (10 oz. protein, 10 oz. fat, 10 oz. of carbohydrates)

Ingredients (4 servings)

1 clove of garlic

4 tablespoon olive oil

8 slices Ciabatta bread

½ bunch small-leaved arugula or rocket

1 tomato

8 slices Serrano ham

1-1 ½ oz. shaved Manchego cheese

Salt and pepper to taste

Preparation

Peel and finely chop the garlic and stir in the oil. Sprinkle the ciabatta slices with garlic oil and roast in a preheated oven (electric stove: 440 ° F / convection: 300 ° F) for about 5 minutes. Let cool down. Wash rocket, shake dry, clean. Wash the tomato, grate to a puree on a coarse grater, and drain on a colander. Brush the bread slices with tomato puree, sprinkle with pepper and a little salt. Top with arugula or rocket, ham, and Manchego. Arrange on a plate.

Pastries and Desserts

Spanish Cortado

Preparation time: 10 min

Nutrition fact (per serving): 400 kcal (8 oz. protein, ½ oz. fat, 10 oz. of carbohydrates)

Ingredients

1 cup sweetened condensed milk

4 cups freshly made espresso

1 cups milk

Ice cubes

Preparation

Divide the ice cubes and condensed milk between four glasses and then carefully pour the espresso on top. Warm up and froth the milk. Pour over and serve immediately.

Spanish Rice Pudding

Preparation time: 15 minutes

Cook time: 45 minutes

Nutrition fact (per serving): 400 kcal (10 oz. protein, ½ oz. fat, 60 oz. of carbohydrates)

Ingredients (4 servings)

1 orange

1 lemon

4½ cup milk

1 pinch salt

1 cinnamon stick

5½ oz. rice pudding

3 ½ oz. sugar

Preparation

Wash both the orange and lemon with hot water and thinly peel about half of the peels with a peeler. Bring the milk and a pinch of salt with the orange and lemon peel, and 1 cinnamon stick to the boil in a large saucepan. Stir in rice pudding and sugar. Bring the rice pudding to the boil briefly and stir. Then turn down the temperature and let the rice pudding swell for 32-35 minutes on medium to low heat. Keep stirring, so that the rice doesn't burn on the bottom of the pot. Turn off the hotplate, put the lid on the pan, and let the rice swell for another 15 minutes on the hotplate. Remove the orange and lemon peel and served with plenty of ground cinnamon.

Spanish Orange Sorbet

Preparation time: 10 minutes

Cook time: 15 minutes

Nutrition fact (per serving): 226 kcal (¼ oz. protein, 40 oz. of carbohydrates)

Ingredients (4 servings)

11 ½ oz. sugar

Grated peel of ½ of the fresh orange

2 cups fresh pressed orange juice

Juice of ½ lemon

1 fluid oz. Campari

Slices of kumquat and mint

Preparation

Bring the sugar, 6 tablespoons of water, and the orange peel to a boil briefly and allow it to cool. Add the orange, lemon juice, and Campari to the sugar solution. Stir everything well and pour it into a metal bowl that's as wide as possible. Place in the freezer. If a layer of ice forms on the surface, stir everything with a whisk. Stir repeatedly until the mixture is smooth and firm. Shape 4 large balls with an ice cream scoop and place it in the freezer for another 14-16 minutes. Arrange the orange sorbet on plates. Garnish with kumquat slices and mint.

Almond Cake with Orange Compote

Preparation time: 25 minutes

Cook time: 40 minutes

Nutrition Fact (per piece): 140 kcal (1 ounce protein, 1½ oz. of fat, 40 oz. of carbohydrates)

Ingredients (4 servings)

5 oranges

12 oz. powdered sugar

2 tablespoons powdered sugar

4 eggs

7 oz. ground almonds with skin

½ teaspoon cinnamon

1 pinch salt

1½ oz. sugar

10 oz. food starch

3 tablespoon vanilla liqueur

Preparation

Wash the orange with hot water, rub dry, and finely grate the peel. Split the orange in half and squeeze out the juice. Sieve 12 oz. of powdered sugar. Separate eggs. Mix egg yolks, 3 oz. powdered sugar, almonds, cinnamon, orange juice, and peel with the whisk of the hand mixer until frothy. Beat the egg whites, 3 oz. powdered sugar, and salt with the hand mixer's whisk until stiff. Pour the egg whites into the almond mixture in two portions. Pour the mixture into a spring form pan (1-inch diameter) lined with baking paper, spread it smoothly, and bake in the preheated oven (electric stove: 300 ° F / convection: 260 ° F) for 32–37 minutes. Remove from the oven and let cool down completely.

For the compote, peel 4 oranges so that the white skin is completely removed. Remove the fillets with a sharp knife from between the separating layers. Squeeze the juice out of the separating membranes and collect it. Boil the sugar with 3 tablespoons of water in a saucepan. Deglaze with the orange juice. Mix the starch with 2 tablespoons of water and liqueur until smooth. Pour into the boiling orange juice and bring to the boil for several seconds while stirring. Remove from the heat, fold in the orange fillets and let cool. Remove the almond cake from the mold, dust with 2 tablespoons of powdered sugar, and cut into 16 pieces. Serve with orange compote.

Spanish Cheesecake Cake

Preparation time: 30 minutes

Cook time: 4 hours

Nutrition Fact (per serving): 515 kcal (½ oz. protein, 30 oz. fat, 40 oz. of carbohydrates)

Ingredients (4 servings)

2 oz. almond kernels with skin

7 oz. cookies with pieces of chocolate

3 oz. butter

3 eggs

2 limes

9 oz. goat cream cheese

14 oz. double cream cheese

1 oz. food starch

5 ½ oz. sugar

52 oz. whipping cream

9 oz. frozen cherries

1/2 can (14 oz.) of sweetened condensed milk

3 ½ oz. cherry jelly

2 packets cream stabilizer

2 packets vanilla sugar

Preparation

Roast the almonds in a pan without fat for 6 minutes. Remove and let them cool down a little and then chop. Place the cookies in a freezer sack and crumble them finely with a rolling pin. Melt the butter in a saucepan and mix with the biscuit crumbs and almonds. Pour into an oiled spring form pan (1 inch diameter) and press down. Chill the biscuit base for approximately 25 minutes. Separate eggs in the meantime. Wash the limes with hot water, rub dry, and peel thinly. Mix both types of cream cheese, egg yolks, starch, lime zest, and 3½ oz. sugar. Beat the egg white until stiff, sprinkling in 2 oz. of sugar.

Beat 5½ oz. cream with the whisk of the hand mixer until stiff. Fold the egg whites and cream one after the other into the cream.

Place two pieces of film approximately 1½ ft. long on the work surface and place another piece of film across them. Place the spring form pan in the middle and pull up the sides with the foil (so that the cake pan is sealed all around with foil). Put the cheese mixture on the dough and smooth it out. Place the spring form pan on the oven pan. Pour boiling water so that 1/3 of the mold is in the water. In the preheated oven (electric stove: 300 ° F / convection: 260 ° F). Bake for 70-90 minutes. Let the cake stand in the switched-off oven with the oven door slightly open for 22–38 minutes, remove from the oven and let cool on a wire rack for 2–3 hours.

Place the condensed milk approximately ½ inch high in an ovenproof casserole dish, close tightly with aluminum foil and place on the drip pan of the oven. Pour boiling water so that half of the baking dish is in the water. Let it caramelize in the preheated oven (electric stove: 440 ° F / convection: 400 ° F) for about 1 hour. Take it out and let it cool down.

Put the cake on a cake plate. Put the jelly in a bowl, stir until smooth and fold in the cherries. Spread the cherry jelly on the cake. Chill the cake for 14-18 minutes. Mix the cream setting agent and vanilla sugar. Briefly beat 14 oz. of whipped cream, slowly pouring in the cream setting. Whip the whipping cream until stiff and use a spoon to spread it loosely over the cherries. Chill the cake for about 30 minutes. Just before serving, stir the dulce de leche until smooth and spread on the cream with a spoon.

Spanish Almond Cake

Preparation time: 45 minutes

Cook time: 45 minutes

Nutrition Fact (per serving): 162 kcal (6¼ oz. protein, ½ oz. fat, 10 oz. of carbohydrates)

Ingredients (4 servings)

1 small untreated orange

1 vanilla pod

4 eggs

3½ oz. sugar

3 oz. ground almonds with skin

3 oz. flour

1 teaspoon baking powder

1 tablespoon almond liqueur

2 pinches of powdered sugar

3 oz. almond flakes

Salt to taste

Preparation

Wash the orange, rub dry and thinly rub the peel. Split the vanilla pod lengthways in half and scrape out the pulp with the back of a knife. Separate 4 eggs. Beat the egg white and 3 tablespoons of cold water with the whisk of the hand mixer until stiff, sprinkling in sugar and salt. Stir in egg yolks, orange peel, vanilla pulp, and liqueur. Mix the almonds, flour, and baking powder, sift in portions onto the egg mixture and fold in. Coat the base of a spring form pan (6 inches diameter) with baking paper. Pour in the sponge cake and smooth it out. Bake in the preheated oven (electric stove: 390 ° F/ convection: 350 ° F) on the middle rack for 22-26 minutes. Sprinkle the almonds on the cake 6 minutes before the baking time and continue baking. Remove the cake from the oven and put it on a wire rack. Remove the cake from the edge of the spring form pan. Allow to cool in the mold, remove. Dust the cake with powdered sugar before serving. Whipped cream tastes good with it.

Spanish Cake with Chorizo and Sheep Cheese

Preparation time: 20 minutes

Cook time: 40 minutes

Nutrition Fact (per piece): 172 kcal (5¼ oz. protein, 10 oz. fat, 10 oz. of carbohydrates)

Ingredients (4 servings)

3 stems basil

11 oz. Chorizo (Spanish paprika sausage)

7 oz. feta cheese

3 oz. butter or margarine

11 oz. flour

1 teaspoon baking powder

3 eggs

3½ oz. creme fraiche cheese

½ cup of milk

3 tablespoons pesto

Salt and pepper to taste

Fat and flour

Preparation

Wash the basil, shake dry, pluck the leaves off, and cut into strips. Cut the Chorizo into pieces. Roughly crumble the feta. Melt fat. Mix the flour and baking powder in a bowl. Whisk eggs, crème fraîche and milk together. Add egg mix, pesto and fat to the flour and stir everything into smooth dough. Finally fold in the chorizo, basil and cheese, season with salt and pepper. Grease the loaf pan (approximately 1½ x ½ inches) and dust with flour. Fill the dough into the mold and bake in the preheated oven (electric stove: 390 ° F/ convection: 350 ° F) for 38-42 minutes. Take the cake out of the oven and let it cool for 15 minutes. Carefully tip the cake from the tin and let it cool down on a wire rack.

Spanish Nougat

Preparation time: 75 minutes

Cook time: 30 minutes

Nutrition Fact (per piece): 80 kcal (¼ oz. protein, ¼ oz. of fat, ¼ oz. of carbohydrates)

Ingredients (10 servings)

5 ½ oz. mixed, candied, exotic fruits (banana, pineapple, mango)

2 oz. whole milk chocolate

7 oz. sugar

3 ½ oz. honey

7 oz. macadamia nuts

7 oz. skinless almonds

5 ½ oz. powdered sugar

6 wafers (4.2 x 7.9 inches)

Parchment paper

Preparation

Roughly chop the candied fruits. Roughly cut the chocolate and melt it in a warm water bath. Boil sugar, honey, and ¾ cup of water in a saucepan to a thick syrup for about 5 minutes. Finely chop the macadamia nuts and almonds. Gradually fold into the syrup. Bring to the boil again and simmer for about 16 minutes. Sift the powdered sugar onto the mixture and fold in. Add chocolate and fruits as well. Roll out the nougat between baking paper into a rectangle (14 x 7.9 inches). Peel off the baking paper on one side and cover with 3 wafers (4.2 x 7.9 inches). Turn the nougat and also cover the other side with wafers. Let cool for 35 minutes. Cut into approximately 60 cubes.

Spanish Apple Pie With Sprinkles

Preparation time: 30 minutes

Cook time: 60 minutes

Nutrition Fact (per serving): 472 kcal (¼ oz. protein, 20¼ oz. fat, 2 oz. of carbohydrates)

Ingredients (8 servings)

42 oz. butter or margarine

52 oz. flour

2 tablespoons cocoa powder

31 oz. sugar

5 sour apples

3 tablespoon lemon juice

1 packet vanilla sugar

4 eggs

1 teaspoon baking powder

2 tablespoons cinnamon

1 tablespoon powdered sugar

3 oz fat

Preparation

Melt 22 oz. of fat. Mix 32 oz. of flour, 1 tablespoon of cocoa, and 11 oz. of sugar. Pour butter on it and knead everything to make crumbles and let cool down. In the meantime, peel and halve the apples and remove the core. Drizzle the apple halves with lemon juice. Mix 7 oz. fat, 7 oz. sugar, and vanilla sugar until creamy. Stir in eggs one at a time. Mix 7 oz. flour, baking powder, 1 tablespoon cinnamon, and 1 tablespoon cocoa.

Stir in the flour mixture, a tablespoon at a time. Pour the dough into a greased spring form pan (6 inches diameter) dusted with flour and smooth it out. Place the apple halves evenly on top. Spread the streusel evenly on the apples.

Bake in a preheated oven (electric stove: 390° F/ convection: 350 ° F) for about 1 hour. Check cake after 45 minutes of baking and cover necessary. Remove the cake from the oven and let it cool on a wire rack. Remove the cake from the edge and dust with 1 tablespoon of cinnamon and powdered sugar.

Spanish Vanilla Cake

Preparation time: 40 minutes

Cook time: 80 minutes

Nutrition Fact (per serving): 365 kcal (¾ oz. protein, 20 oz. fat, 1 oz. of carbohydrates)

Ingredients (8 servings)

3 ½ oz. butter or margarine

10½ oz. dark chocolate couverture

14 oz. raw marzipan paste

1 vanilla pod

1 pinch salt

8 eggs

3½ oz. sugar

3½ oz. flour

20¼ oz. ground almonds without skin

1 tablespoon powdered sugar

Green food coloring

Preparation

Melt the fat and let it cool down. Chop 5½ oz. couverture. Finely grate marzipan. Cut the vanilla pod lengthways and scrape out the pulp. Add the vanilla pulp to the marzipan. Add salt. Separate the eggs and add the yolks as well. Mix the marzipan mixture with the whisk of the hand mixer until creamy. Beat the egg white in 2 portions until stiff, gradually pour in the sugar. Stir 1/3 of the egg whites into the marzipan cream. Sift the flour. Alternate the flour, almonds, liquid fat, and 1/3 of the egg whites under the mixture. Fold in the remaining egg whites. Place 1/3 of the dough into a spring form pan (6 inches diameter) that has been greased and dusted with flour and smooth out. Scatter half of the chopped couverture on top. Put 1/3 of the dough on top, smooth it out and sprinkle with the remaining couverture. Cover with the other batter and smooth out. Bake in a warmed-up oven (electric stove: 350 ° F / convection: 300 ° F) for about 45 minutes. Take out the cake of the oven and let it cool down on a wire rack. Knead 3 oz. of marzipan and food coloring and use them to form bells of various sizes. Roughly chop 5½ oz. couverture and melt in a hot water bath. Cover the cake with couverture and let it dry for 40 minutes.

Spanish Saffron Wreaths

Preparation time: 30 minutes

Cook time: 60 minutes

Nutrition fact (per serving): 190 kcal (½ oz. protein, 1½ oz. of fat, 30 oz. of carbohydrates)

Ingredients (4 servings)

1 jar or packets of ground saffron

13 oz. butter

3 oz. sugar

1 packet vanilla sugar

1 egg

12 oz. flour

1 pinch baking powder

5¼ oz. powdered sugar

1¼ oz. chopped or 3 oz. halved pistachio nuts

2 pieces of cling film

2 parchment papers

1 small freezer bag

Preparation

Dissolve the saffron in 1 teaspoon of hot water. Mix the butter, sugar and vanilla sugar with the whisk of the hand mixer until creamy. Stir in the egg and saffron. Mix and knead the flour and baking powder. Wrap the dough in foil and refrigerate for at least 1 hour. Roll out the dough 1/6 inch thick on a floured work surface. Using a round cutter (3-inch diameter) with a wavy edge, cut out the plates and place on 3-4 baking sheets lined with baking paper. Cut out the middle of the pastry sheets with a smooth, round cutter (1½ inches diameter) and lift out. Knead the leftover dough together, roll out again and cut out wreaths as described. Bake the trays one after the other in the preheated oven (electric stove: 350 ° F / convection: 300 ° F) for about 11 minutes. Remove the wreaths from the baking sheet with the baking paper and leave to cool on wire racks. For decoration, mix 3 tablespoons of hot water and powdered sugar to a smooth glaze. Pour the casting into a small freezer bag, cut off a small corner, and spray the casting onto the wreaths in a loop. Place the pistachios in the loops and press lightly.

Spanish Cherry Marzipan Cake

Preparation time: 105 minutes

Cook time: 2 hours

Nutrition Fact (per serving): 520 kcal (10 oz. protein, 1 oz. fat, 50¼ oz. of carbohydrates)

Ingredients (6 servings)

10 oz. butter

5 ¼ oz. dark chocolate couverture

31 ¾ oz. raw marzipan paste

8 eggs

1 vanilla pod

1 pinch of salt

8 1/2oz sugar

3½ oz. flour

20 oz. ground almonds

1 packet "Vanilla flavor" pudding powder

2¼ cups of milk

18 oz. cherries

1 packet red fruit jelly (raspberry flavor)

1¼ sour cherry juice

Preparation

Melt the butter and let it cool. Chop the couverture, finely grated 10½ oz. of marzipan—separate eggs. Mix the marzipan, vanilla pulp, salt, and egg yolks with the whisk of the hand mixer until creamy. Beat the egg white in 2 portions until stiff; gradually pour in 3½ oz. of sugar. Stir 1/3 of the egg whites into the marzipan cream. Mix in the flour, almonds, butter, and 1/3 of the egg whites alternately. Fold in the remaining egg whites. Pour 1/3 of the dough into a greased springform pan (6 inches diameter) dusted with flour, smooth out. Spread half of the chopped couverture on top. Put 1/3 of the dough on top, smooth it out and sprinkle with the remaining couverture. Spread the rest of the batter on top.

Bake in a preheated oven (electric stove: 350 ° F / convection: 300 ° F) for about 40 minutes. Allow to cool on a grill. Mix the pudding powder, 2 oz. of sugar, and 6 tablespoons milk until smooth. Add the rest milk to the boil, stir in the mixed powder, cook for 1 minute. Let cool a little and fill on the bottom. Put in the fridge for 40 minutes. In the meantime, wash the cherries. Mix the red groats powder, 3 oz. sugar, and 6 tablespoons cherry nectar until smooth. Bring the remaining juice and 1 cup of water to the boil, stir in the mixed red grits powder, and cook for 1 minute. Fold in the cherries and distribute on top of the cake. Chill for 1 hour. To decorate, knead 1 2/3 oz. of marzipan and roll out thinly between 2 layers of foil. Cut out the flowers and turn them in 1 tablespoon of sugar. Cut the cake into sizes and decorate with the marzipan flowers Stir in the mixed powder, cook for 1 minute. Let cool a little and fill on the bottom. Cool it in the fridge for 40 minutes, before serving.

Spanish Liqueur Curls

Preparation time: 90 minutes

Cook time: 30 minutes

Nutrition Fact (per serving): 720 kcal (½ oz. protein, 1½ oz. of fat, 2¾ oz. of carbohydrates)

Ingredients (5 servings)

9 oz. flour

4 leveled tablespoons of crème fraîche

9 oz. cold butter

5 ¼ oz. powdered sugar

8 tablespoon Spanish liqueur

Sugar pearls

Parchment paper

Preparation

Put the flour, crème fraîche, and butter in a mixing bowl. Knead with the hand mixer's dough hook, then quickly with cool hands to form smooth dough. Roll the dough to an approximately thickness of 1/5 inches on a work surface well dusted with flour. Cut out circles with a rascal cutter (about 2 inches). Place on 3 baking sheets lined with baking paper. Bake one after the other in a preheated oven (electric stove: 350 ° F / convection: 300 ° F) for 17-21 minutes. Let it cool down. Mix the powdered sugar and liqueur to a smooth glaze. Spread it on the rings. Sprinkle with granulated sugar and sugar pearls.

Turrones

Preparation time: 20 minutes

Cook time: 20 minutes

Nutrition Fact (per serving): 250 kcal (50 oz. protein, 10 oz. of fat, 50 oz. of carbohydrates)

Ingredients (5 servings)

14 oz. almonds

22 oz. icing sugar

3 tablespoons of cocoa powder

2 oz. honey

3 proteins

Vanilla pod

12 large rectangular wafers

Preparation

Bring a pot of water to the boil, add the almonds, and cook for 2 minutes. Drain the almonds in a colander and rinse with cold water. Peel off the almonds' skins and place them on kitchen paper until they've dried. Preheat the oven to 390 F. Spread the almonds on a baking sheet and roast them until golden brown. Let them cool down. Put half of the almonds aside, grind the other half in a food processor, or first put in a freezer bag, roughly chop with a rolling pin and then grind into powder by hand in a mortar. Put the egg whites in a bowl, add the vanilla pulp (from the vanilla pod) and beat the mixture very stiff. Finally, add the cocoa powder and whisk in.

Add some water in a large saucepan and bring to a boil. Place a smaller saucepan in the larger saucepan, add the honey and heat until the honey is liquid. Gradually add the icing sugar while constantly stirring. Add the ground almonds and continue stirring. Remove the pot from the oven. Finally, slowly add the protein mixture to the honey mixture and stir well.

Line a baking sheet completely with wafers, so that the wafers are close together and there are no gaps between them. Put the turrones mixture on the wafers and spread evenly. Place the wafers close together on top of the mixture. Place a layer of parchment paper on top of the wafers and a baking sheet to weigh down. Let the turrones set for at least 1 day and cut into 1¼ x 2½ inches pieces the next day.

Churros

Preparation time: 45 minutes

Cook time: 45 minutes

Nutrition Fact (per servings): 425 kcal (10 oz. protein, 6 oz. of fat, 6 oz. of carbohydrates)

Ingredients (6 servings)

1¼ cup water

3½ oz. butter

4 eggs

1 pinch salt

7 oz. flour

4 cups frying oil

2 oz. icing sugar

22 oz. dark chocolate

Preparation

Add water to the pan and add the butter and bring to the boil briefly until the butter has dissolved. Add the salt. Add the flour and stir with a wooden spoon until the dough separates from the edge of the pan and forms thick dough. Transfer the dough to a bowl and let it cool. Stir in the eggs one by one with a wooden spoon until a creamy batter is formed.

Heat the fat in a saucepan to 360 ° F. Equip a piping bag with a star nozzle and pour in the choux pastry. Inject long strips into the hot fat. Cut off the spout with scissors. Fry the churros for 2-3 minutes, lift out with a slotted spoon, and degrease on kitchen paper. Let them cool and dust with powdered sugar or granulated sugar.

Almond Biscuits

Preparation time: 20 minutes

Cook time: 25 minutes

Nutrition fact (per serving): 490 kcal (10 ounces protein, 3 ounces fat, 15 ounces of carbohydrates)

Ingredients (1 serving)

7 oz. flour

7 oz. sugar

4 eggs

3 ½ oz. almonds

Preparation

Preheat the oven to 320 F and line a baking sheet with baking paper. Knead some dough out of flour, sugar, eggs, and almonds on a work surface. Roll this out on the baking sheet 1/2-inch-thick and prebake in the oven for 12 minutes. Then cut the dough into finger-length strips and bake for 14-17 minutes.

For any $2,99 you can buy other cookbooks with 111 recipes from Italy, Greece, Iran, Armenia, Romania, Turkey, Syria and many more...

Available at Amazon, the full list is available at www.balkanfood.org/cook-books/

If you liked Spanish food, discover to how cook DELICIOUS recipes from Balkan countries!

Within these pages, you'll learn 35 authentic recipes from a Balkan cook. These aren't ordinary recipes you'd find on the Internet, but recipes that were closely guarded by our Balkan mothers and passed down from generation to generation.

Main Dishes, Appetizers, and Desserts included!

If you want to learn how to make Croatian green peas stew, and 32 other authentic Balkan recipes, then start with our book!

If you're a Mediterranean dieter who wants to know the secrets of the Mediterranean diet, dieting, and cooking, then you're about to discover how to master cooking meals on a Mediterranean diet right now!

In fact, if you want to know how to make Mediterranean food, then this new e-book - "The 30-minute Mediterranean diet" - gives you the answers to many important questions and challenges every Mediterranean dieter faces, including:

- How can I succeed with a Mediterranean diet?
- What kind of recipes can I make?
- What are the key principles to this type of diet?
- What are the suggested weekly menus for this diet?
- Are there any cheat items I can make?

... and more!

If you're serious about cooking meals on a Mediterranean diet and you really want to know how to make Mediterranean food, then you need to grab a copy of "The 30-minute Mediterranean diet" right now.

Prepare **111 recipes with several ingredients in less than 30 minutes!**

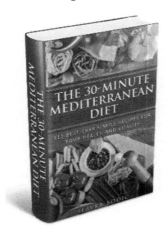

What could be better than a home-cooked meal? Maybe only a Greek homemade meal.

Do not get discouraged if you have no Greek roots or friends.

Now you can make a Greek food feast in your kitchen.

This ultimate Greek cookbook offers you 111 best dishes of this cuisine! From more famous gyros to more exotic Kota Kapama this cookbook keeps it easy and affordable.

All the ingredients necessary are wholesome and widely accessible.

The author's picks are as flavorful as they are healthy. The dishes described in this cookbook are "what Greek mothers have made for decades."

Full of well-balanced and nutritious meals, this handy cookbook includes many vegan options.

Discover a plethora of benefits of Mediterranean cuisine, and you may fall in love with cooking at home.

Inspired by a real food lover, this collection of delicious recipes will taste buds utterly satisfied.

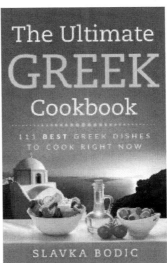

Maybe to try exotic Serbian cuisine?

From succulent sarma, soups, warm and cold salads to delectable desserts, the plethora of flavors will satisfy the most jaded foodie. Have a taste of a new culture with this **traditional Serbian cookbook**.

ONE LAST THING

If you enjoyed this book or found it useful I'd be very grateful if you could find the time to post a short review on Amazon. Your support really does make a difference and I read all the reviews personally, so I can get your feedback and make this book even better.

Thanks again for your support!

Please send me your feedback at

www.balkanfood.org

Printed in Great Britain
by Amazon

14206554R00131